Praise for *Why Loyalty Matters*

"This is a supremely practical book with a profoundly moral message: that the quality of our lives, the productivity of our organizations, and the depth of our relationships are inextricably related. This book should not be used only as a guide for leaders, but as a guide for life."

—Joseph Grenny, *New York Times* Bestselling Co-Author of *Influencer: The Power to Change Anything* and *Crucial Conversations: Tools for Talking When Stakes are High*

"*Why Loyalty Matters* is a wonderful, timely book. Reading it can improve your relationships, your work, and actually make you happier."

—Tal-Ben Shahar, *New York Times* Bestselling Author of *Happier*

"*Why Loyalty Matters* is fun to read, practical to do, and invaluable to your success."

—Keith Ferrazzi, *New York Times* Bestselling Author of *Never Eat Alone*

"The idea of loyalty is much more than a platitude, it is the foundation by which people develop successful businesses and happy lives. Anyone who seeks to cultivate loyal customers, employees, and loved ones should not only read this book, but mark it up as a reference guide."

—Adrian Gostick and Chester Elton, *New York Times* Bestselling Authors of *The Carrot Principle*

"Keiningham and Aksoy have written the definitive book on the what, how, and why of loyalty."

—Sonja Lyubomirsky, Bestselling Author of
The How of Happiness, and Professor of Psychology
at the University of California, Riverside

"In good times loyalty is important; in challenging times it's essential. *Why Loyalty Matters* is the best book on loyalty ever written."

—Michael Watkins, Bestselling Author of *The First 90 Days:
Critical Success Strategies for New Leaders at All Levels*
and Co-founder of Genesis Advisers

"Loyalty matters! It's so direct and fundamental that we lose sight of just how important it really is. Keiningham and Aksoy brilliantly illustrate that the key to lasting success and happiness—in all parts of life, not just work—hinges on our human ability to be loyal. The message of *Why Loyalty Matters* is timeless—and timely."

—Stewart Friedman, Bestselling Author of *Total Leadership:
Be a Better Leader, Have a Richer Life* and Professor of
Management at the University of Pennsylvania's
Wharton School

"We are a species for whom meaningful connections to others are essential for our health and happiness. This wonderful book makes the important point that for social connections to be meaningful and to make us happy and healthy, they cannot be fleeting, and that loyalty is a key ingredient of a life lived well."

—John Cacioppo, Bestselling Co-Author of *Loneliness*,
Distinguished Professor of Psychology at the University
of Chicago, and Past President of the Association
for Psychological Science

"Loyalty is a key ingredient in creating a high-performance culture. Those leaders, athletes, or coaches who can leverage the power of loyalty have a distinct home field advantage. *Why Loyalty Matters* is the first playbook of its kind."
—David Kasiarz, Senior Vice President,
Global Compensation and Benefits, American Express

"As the CEO of 2,400 employees ranging from veterans to boomers, Xers to Nexters, it is challenging to understand motivation and engagement. *Why Loyalty Matters* is a brilliant and thought-provoking book that not only identifies issues, but also provides real-life answers. In a complicated world, it is an excellent resource to utilize with struggling individuals and teams, and I was challenged to consider my own motivations and behaviors that influence my personal happiness and satisfaction."
—Britt Berrett, President & CEO, Medical City &
Medical City Children's Hospital, Dallas, TX

"What makes the final difference in personal and professional relationships? Loyalty is the difference maker! Tim and Lerzan remind us that personal qualities always transcend the technical!"
—Bob Beaudine, Bestselling Author of *The Power of WHO*,
and President & CEO of Eastman & Beaudine

"*Why Loyalty Matters* powerfully demonstrates a fundamental truth that we forget all too often—that it is indeed good business to be good to one another."
—Rita G. McGrath, Professor of Management at
Columbia University, Consultant, and Bestselling
Co-Author of *Discovery-Driven Growth*

"*Why Loyalty Matters* provides exceptional insight into the nuances of loyalty, and how to achieve the right kind. This book will be of great interest to all who seek to enhance their well-being through loyalty."

—Ajay K. Kohli, Professor of Marketing
at the Georgia Institute of Technology,
and Editor of the *Journal of Marketing*

"It is a paradox that with increased quality of life, fewer people seem to be truly happy. Contrary to popular thinking, no man is an island! In *Why Loyalty Matters*, the authors make a brilliant case of linking loyalty to happiness. To improve our individual and collective happiness we need to rethink our caring for other people. The reward is the mutual joy of being included into something big and enriching."

—Tor W. Andreassen, Professor and Chair
of the Department of Marketing,
BI Norwegian School of Management

"This is a fun and fascinating book that is almost impossible to put down, and it provides solutions to a critical problem. If you want to be a better friend, spouse, manager, employee, customer, citizen of the world—or if you just want to be happier—please read this book!"

—Bruce Cooil, Professor of Management, Owen
Graduate School of Management, Vanderbilt University

"At a time when some corporate executives raked in millions of dollars while laying off many of their most loyal, long-term employees—with some pundits proclaiming that's just fine—it's time for a book that spells out exactly 'Why Loyalty Matters.' I hope that every CEO in the world reads this book."

—Roland Rust, Distinguished Professor of Marketing, University of Maryland, and Bestselling Author of *Customer Equity Management*

"This book generates insightful information about all types of loyalty and provides compelling arguments for why loyalty is important in all walks of life. A lot of analytical thinking has gone into the writing of this book. A must-read for everyone."

—V. Kumar, Distinguished Professor of Marketing, Georgia State University, and Bestselling Author of *Managing Customers for Profit*

"*Why Loyalty Matters* offers a fascinating analysis of the many facets of loyalty. Anyone interested in enhancing his or her quality of life (and who isn't?) will enjoy reading and benefit immensely from this well-researched, wonderfully crafted, and engaging book."

—A. "Parsu" Parasuraman, Vice Dean of Faculty and Professor of Marketing, University of Miami, and Editor of the *Journal of Service Research*

"This very week, an interviewer for a trade publication asked me, 'Why should our readers care about loyalty?' Tim Keiningham and Lerzan Aksoy deeply and thoroughly answer this oft-asked question in surprising, memorable, and provocative ways. *Why Loyalty Matters* is one of those rare books that teaches profound business, life, and history lessons simultaneously. Read it and be inspired."

—Jill Griffin, Bestselling Author of *Taming the Search-and-Switch Customer* and *Customer Loyalty: How To Earn It, How To Keep It*

"*Why Loyalty Matters* looks at loyalty in bold, new ways. By taking both a broad and deep view of loyalty—and how it affects our life, our work, and our societies, Keiningham and Aksoy have provided a promising roadmap for our future. Timely, useful, and fun to read!"

—Katherine Lemon, Professor of Marketing, Boston College, and Editor of the *Journal of Service Research* (beginning June 1, 2009)

Why Loyalty Matters

Why Loyalty Matters

*The Groundbreaking Approach to
Rediscovering Happiness, Meaning,
and Lasting Fulfillment in Your Life and Work*

Timothy Keiningham and Lerzan Aksoy
with Luke Williams

BENBELLA BOOKS, INC.
Dallas, TX

BENBELLA

BenBella Books, Inc.
6440 N. Central Expressway, Suite 503
Dallas, TX 75206
www.benbellabooks.com
Send feedback to feedback@benbellabooks.com

Printed in the United States of America
10 9 8 7 6 5 4 3 2 1

Library of Congress Cataloging-in-Publication Data is available for this title.
ISBN 978-1933771-72-4

Proofreading by Stacia Seaman and Erica Lovett
Cover design by Todd Michael Bushman
Text design and composition by PerfecType, Nashville, TN
Printed by Bang Printing

Distributed by Perseus Distribution
perseusdistribution.com

To place orders through Perseus Distribution:
Tel: 800-343-4499
Fax: 800-351-5073
E-mail: orderentry@perseusbooks.com

Significant discounts for bulk sales are available. Please contact Glenn Yeffeth at glenn@benbellabooks.com or (214) 750-3628.

To those who truly believe that we all matter, and who seek to make the world a better place by acting like we do.

✹ ✹ ✹

Lack of loyalty is one of the major causes of failure in every walk of life.

—Napoleon Hill (1883–1970), excerpted from *Think and Grow Rich* (originally published in 1937—arguably the bestselling success book of all time)

✹ ✹ ✹

Hana Keiningham, Sage Keiningham, Alexander Keiningham, Christopher Keiningham, and Deren Kurtay . . . we do this in the hope that you will grow up in a world surrounded by loving, loyal friends.

Contents

Preface

This book is about a very simple idea. *Why Loyalty Matters* makes the case that loyalty is critical to our happiness as individuals and our health as a society, that loyalty improves the performance of our businesses and our satisfaction as employees. We argue that at some point our culture decided that loyalty was an old-fashioned and unimportant virtue, and that this decision has made us weaker as a society and less satisfied as individuals.

But this isn't a book of philosophy. Our goal is to help every reader gain significant personal insight into the role loyalty plays in his and her life. In order to do this, we have developed LoyaltyAdvisor™, a powerful tool that allows you to assess your relationship style and examine your loyalties across multiple areas that have been proven to correlate to happiness. Even more, LoyaltyAdvisor allows your friends and associates to assess your loyalty across multiple dimensions, providing you with objective, confidential, third-party feedback. On the reverse side of the dust jacket of this book you'll find a one-time-use code that you can use to gain access to LoyaltyAdvisor. We believe that you will find this tool very helpful.

We've been thinking and writing about loyalty for some time now. We co-wrote the award-winning book *Loyalty Myths*, which focused on loyalty in relationship to business performance. *Why Loyalty Matters* takes a broader perspective, examining the role loyalty plays in our lives as businesspeople and employees, husbands and wives, friends and citizens.

We recognize that, like any virtue, loyalty can go too far and become toxic, and we discuss how to recognize and avoid these situations. But overall, we believe that we are a society that undervalues loyalty, and we examine the issues of loyalty and faith, how loyalty can be taught, and how it can become an increasingly important part of our society. We're hopeful that this book can be part of a growing movement that recognizes the importance of the fundamental values of life, loyalty chief among them.

We hope you can be part of this movement as well!

Chapter 1

The Why of Loyalty

A happiness that is sought for ourselves alone can never be found; for a happiness that is diminished by being shared is not big enough to make us happy.

—Thomas Merton (1915–1968),
Catholic monk and author,
No Man Is an Island

1

We need one another. If history has shown us anything, it is that our ability to work together has ensured our continued existence. But our connection to one another is about much more than our physical survival. We need one another to be whole: physically, emotionally, and spiritually. And research consistently shows that we need one another to be happy.

Unfortunately, for too many of us, connections to family, friends, lovers, and communities have stretched into thin, easily snapped threads. Pulled in every direction, we find no time in our fast-paced, hectic schedules to devote to the people and causes that fill us up emotionally and spiritually.

At some point, virtually all of us have felt this way. While we may shudder in the moment, we ultimately shake it off, taking solace in the fact that we are fundamentally okay, right here and right now. We're not suffering oppressive tyranny right now. Society isn't collapsing right now, at this very moment. Our governments are slow to act and sometimes fail to do right by us, but we're not dying because of it. We aren't dying from relationships that seem to exist only as tests of will, as emotional roller coasters. There are things wrong with the world, with our country, with our work, and with ourselves, but we're okay. Right here and right now, we're okay.

No, we're not okay. Sure, we aren't facing imminent death. But for most of us, life is far from perfect. Almost none of us—less than 5 percent—strongly agree with this statement: "I am completely satisfied with my life." In fact, even if you combine this 5 percent with the next highest rating, that number is still only around 15 percent. That's fewer than two out of ten of us!

This finding isn't so surprising when you think about how we divide up our days. Research shows the majority of us believe that we aren't allocating the right amount of time between family, friends, and work.

I feel that the amount of time and effort I give to my family/friends/company is about right.

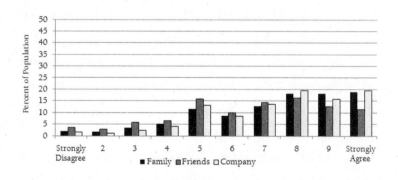

Source: Ipsos Loyalty

Solving this problem isn't as simple as time management. It is more deeply rooted. As a society, we are losing the sense of one of the most important principles in our lives, all because we've simply fallen out of practice. The principle that binds us together is loyalty.

Without us noticing it, the world has shifted from a society of many long-term loyalties to a society of transactional relationships and ephemeral contacts. This is a natural by-product of the increasingly dynamic economic environment in which we live. We have become more flexible and more mobile workers, which has made businesses more efficient. And this has given us greater opportunities to succeed, making us wealthier.

But it has also made us less loyal. Because successful organizations are built on relationships, this actually isn't good for business. And it isn't good for us as individuals either—it definitely has not made us happier!

Times Have Changed

Historically, loyalty wasn't optional. Ostracism represented the ultimate disgrace. Why would early settlers in the American colonies tolerate public humiliation, such as being put on display in medieval stocks? Why not simply leave the group? Because leaving was even more unpalatable. It meant no support, emotionally or physically, from the community. And no support most likely meant an early death.

But times have changed dramatically. Leaving the group seldom risks one's survival today. The prosperity of the modern era has also provided us with greater opportunities. These opportunities bring with them the greater likelihood that we will shift our loyalties in search of greener pastures. As a result, leaving the group has become the increasingly popular option when we object to the actions or positions in a community.

Columbia University law professor George P. Fletcher observes, "In the marketplace, where all that is at stake is the performance of the product or the quality of the service, the best thing to do is leave—that is, to find the competitor who better supplies the needed good. The exemplar of the marketplace has conquered neighboring arenas. Today we think about relatives, employers, religious groups, and nations the way we think about companies that supply us with other products and services. If we don't like what we are getting, we consider the competition."

Without question, "voting with your feet" is the ultimate punishment that we as individuals can exact on a community. It actually threatens the viability of any society. If enough people leave, the group is forced to change, disintegrate, or in the worst of cases, hold people hostage. This last was the case in East Germany; the loss of so many of its citizens caused the government to erect the Berlin Wall— not to keep enemies out, but to force its citizens to stay.

While we often think of "leaving" in economic "customer–company" or political "government–citizen" relationships, the possibility of leaving applies to some degree to our relationships with everyone. Weak friendships, dysfunctional families, bad marriages, intolerant religious institutions, and inept governments all face the prospect of abandonment. And there are indeed times when leaving is the best option.

But society cannot function and relationships cannot last if leaving is the readily selected, probable outcome to every perceived grievance. And while few would admit to cutting and running when times get tough, many, if not most of us, have a general sense that leaving has become too easy for many.

Cicero, ancient Rome's greatest orator, observed more than two thousand years ago: "What is the quality to look out for as a warrant for the stability and permanence of friendship? It is Loyalty. Nothing that lacks this can be stable." This isn't just true of friendships. Loyalty is the cornerstone of stability in all of our relationships.

The fundamental assumption of leaving is that life is better without that relationship. The problem is that in a world of easily shifting loyalties, we are likely to find ourselves surrounded by fair-weather friends. As the bonds of friendship and community become ever more tenuous, we find loyal companions more difficult to attain. As a result, stability in our lives and work becomes increasingly difficult to maintain.

Loyalty Is Dead

You can count me as an out-of-date dinosaur. I come from an era when loyalty and gratitude were regally honored. . . . In a strange way, loyalty is now seen as some kind of a character flaw.
—Jack Valenti (1921–2007), president of the Motion Picture Association of America, 1966–2004

From the dawn of civilization, the great works of literature are almost universally tales of loyalty and betrayal. To the ancient Greeks, a hero could not exist apart from loyalty. Tests of loyalty are the cornerstone of great drama. We revere the sacrifices of friends, lovers, patriots, and religious icons in their loyalty to great causes. And we reserve our utmost contempt for the traitors who betray their loyalty for personal gain—a Judas!

Or at least we used to do so.

Loyalty is now out of fashion—an anachronism worthy of derision in today's rapidly changing environment. Loyalty is frequently spoken of as a character flaw. Paul Begala, a former advisor to President Bill Clinton, observes, "We have a media culture that derides loyalty, sees it as phony, looks for an ulterior motive, or at best is patronizing about it."

One only need look at the comments of former U.S. President Jimmy Carter to see how far loyalty has fallen out of favor. When asked to describe how he viewed British Prime Minister Tony Blair's support of U.S. President George W. Bush, Carter replied: "Abominable. Loyal. Blind. Apparently subservient."

OUCH! A former U.S. president and Nobel Peace Prize laureate treats the word *loyal* as an insult.

He is not alone. It is not difficult to find articles declaring that loyalty is either dead or on life support. And the statistics bear this out. On average, companies lose half of their customers within five years. And employees leave at an even faster rate; on average, a company loses half of its employees within four years. Job-hopping has become the norm. Younger baby boomers (those born between 1957 and 1964) held 9.6 jobs on average—without question, far more jobs than those of their parents and grandparents. The idea of spending a lifetime with a company is as old-fashioned as families sitting around the radio.

And companies have shown equal disdain for the idea. We've all heard, "Our employees are our greatest asset," yet our own experiences tell us that far too often these words are an empty slogan. While touring one of Scott Paper's plants, an employee proudly told then-CEO Al Dunlap that he was a thirty-year veteran. Dunlap's loyalty-critical reply? "Why would you stay with a company for thirty years?"

Although few CEOs are as callous as Dunlap, CEOs frequently have short tenures with the companies they oversee. Furthermore, their primary loyalty is supposed to be to the shareholders. While there is nothing inherently wrong with this, all too often the focus on shareholders is translated into a focus on near-term profits rather than on what is in the best long-term interest of the company.

The result? Downsizing has become the prevalent means of reengineering the corporation. Once-loyal employees are told *en masse* that the company's loyalty to them is no longer economically viable. And shareholders have typically responded with increases in the stock price when downsizings are announced.

Yet disloyalty does not end at the corporate offices. We take traces of this disloyalty home with us, until it slowly begins to permeate all aspects of our society from the small interactions to life-altering ones.

The harsh face of disloyalty bombards us every day. In fact, tabloid journalism thrives in large part because of the ease with which (former) friends are willing to sell unflattering stories and pictures of their now-famous friends. And tell-all books line the bestseller lists. Clearly, society is eager to reward such disloyalty by providing it with a lucrative market.

What's the Big Deal?

Does it really matter that we are becoming less loyal as a society? And what difference does loyalty make to my happiness? As Professor Andreas Kinneging rhetorically asks:

> Maybe there is little loyalty, little sense of a "we," little community. But we have other things. We have an unprecedented liberty of the individual, the "I," to do whatever it wants with whomever it wants to do it. And what we lack in terms of community, loyalty, and trust, we can make good with our unmatched spending power—by buying insurance, legal aid, police protection, etc. Who needs loyalty anymore?

The problem? A disloyal society is a selfish society; a society of loyalty only to oneself is the antithesis of loyalty. Loyalty—once priceless—now dies with economic opportunism. As a well-worn joke laments, "It's difficult to determine which is worse: that we sell our principles or that we sell them so cheaply."

Still, few will admit that they are not loyal. In fact, we tend to believe that we are very loyal. But we don't believe that we are surrounded by loyal friends.

I am a loyal friend vs. I have many loyal friends.

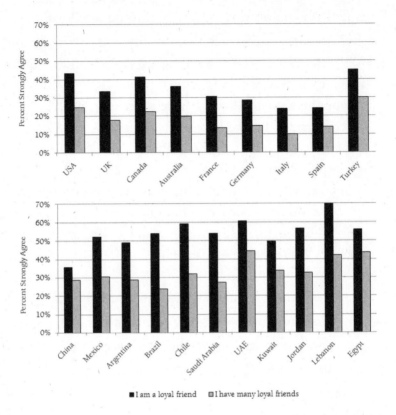

■ I am a loyal friend   ▣ I have many loyal friends

Source: Ipsos Loyalty

This presents us with a paradox. How can the world be filled with loyal people, yet we are not surrounded by loyal friends? Clearly, only one of these things can be true; either we are less loyal than we admit or our friends are more loyal than we believe them to be.

Research shows that we tend to view our partners as being much less loyal to us than we believe we are to them.

And, of course, our partners view their loyalty to us to be far greater than our loyalty to them.

So which is more likely to be true? Are the vast majority of us underappreciated loyalists? Or are we biased judges of our own loyalty? In our hearts, we all know the answer. It's very hard to be objective about ourselves, particularly when it involves assessing our own character.

A Turkish proverb says, "Show me your friends, and I'll show you who you are." Our friends act as mirrors of the people we are. We tend to surround ourselves with others like ourselves. If we don't see our friends as fiercely loyal, then the odds are that we aren't either.

The problem with our lack of objectivity is that we tend to see problems of loyalty only in others. In other words, we see the speck in our brother's eye but fail to notice the beam in our own eye. No one says, "I am not loyal." And no one fixes a problem that they refuse to acknowledge they have.

What Is Loyalty Anyway?

When loyalty is absent, ideals are barren.

—Lawrence Pearsall Jacks (1860–1955),
English educator, philosopher, and author

In our youth, loyalty was easy to identify. Did you stand by and stick up for your friends? Did you keep their secrets? Did you make sure that no one bullied your brother or sister? There was no *sort of* loyal. You were loyal, or you weren't.

As adults, loyalty is not nearly so simple. We operate in a network of overlapping loyalties. Some loyalties are trivial. Other loyalties provide the foundation to our very identity.

Paradoxically, while we all value loyalty in our friends, our sense of what loyalty actually means tends to be vague. American political consultant James Carville observes:

> Dogs are famously loyal . . . but that's not loyalty; that's obedience. Nor is it the "omertà" stuff you see in Mafia movies. People don't seem to appreciate that there's a difference between being loyal and being a sycophant or an idiot. The sycophant has an easy job. He or she just determines who's in power and then sucks up to them . . . and an idiot's just an idiot.

Carville is absolutely correct. Real loyalty is not about submission, sucking up, or surrendering your intelligence to follow the will of another blindly.

So what exactly does it mean to be "loyal"? Loyalty is about accepting the bonds that our relationships with others entail, and acting in a way that defends and reinforces the attachment inherent in these relationships. A simpler way to think about it is this: *Loyalty is the counterpart to the word "my"!*

We can be loyal to many things—friend, lover, family, church, community, country, employer, store, and restaurant (just to name a few). And some loyalties can be more important to us than others. Yet in all cases, loyalty implies a specialness of the relationship. What makes it special is our identification with the object of our loyalty—at some level, we think of it as belonging to us. As Fletcher puts it, "There comes a point at which logic runs dry and one must plant one's loyalty in the simple fact that it is *my* friend, *my* club, *my* alma mater, *my* nation." Amen!

The word "my" implies psychological ownership. We "own" things because they bring value to our lives; otherwise, we would discard them. But ownership is about more than deriving pleasure. Ownership demands responsibility. When a relationship falls into the category of "my," that responsibility is our loyalty.

Being Happy

To a large degree, our issues with loyalty arise because we don't see the direct connection between loyalty and happiness. And we all want to be happy, even if we may not want to admit it. In fact, we have come to believe that being happy is an unchallengeable right, enshrined in the U.S. Declaration of Independence.

> We hold these truths to be self-evident, that all men are created equal, that they are endowed by their Creator with certain unalienable Rights, that among these are Life, Liberty and the pursuit of Happiness.

When Thomas Jefferson wrote these words in the Declaration of Independence, the idea of a right to pursue happiness was revolutionary.

While humans have always understood what it means to be happy, for most of our existence we didn't think that it was the normal condition. For most of the last two thousand years, life for the vast majority was so extraordinarily difficult that the idea of a "right" to pursue happiness never occurred to most people.

Princeton University professor Robert Darnton refers to "the human condition as it was experienced by most people for . . . two thousand years, when men and women worked the fields in a state of semi-slavery, ate little more than bread and broth, and died young. Theirs was an existence best summed up by Thomas Hobbes' description of life in the state of nature: 'solitary, poor, nasty, brutish, and short.'"

At the time, the pursuit of happiness was a life in search of spiritual salvation: a life of suffering with the hope of an afterlife in Paradise. It was not until the Age of Enlightenment was combined with improved living conditions that people began to believe that happiness might be attainable in this life. Achieving happiness has gone from being unfathomable to being the primary goal in life.

We live in an era of unprecedented opportunity to enhance the quality of our lives and to pursue happiness. In general, we are wealthier, healthier, worldlier, better educated, better fed, and better entertained than our parents and grandparents. By almost any standard we use to measure prosperity, we are better off than at any time in history.

So this raises a question: "Are we having fun yet?" Given that improved economic conditions were critical in our belief in a "right" to happiness, you would think that people are happier than they were fifty years ago—after all, our standards of living have risen dramatically over that time.

We are more prosperous than our parents and grandparents.

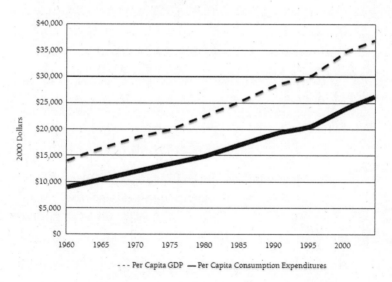

Source: U.S. Bureau of the Census, Statistical Abstract of the United States: 2006 (Washington, D.C., 2006) p. 448.

The truth is that if you look back to 1946 (when formal "happiness" surveys began in the United States), the percentage of people reporting that they are very happy hasn't increased at all. And this isn't just an American trend; it's true across most developed countries.

Average Happiness in the World (1946–2006)

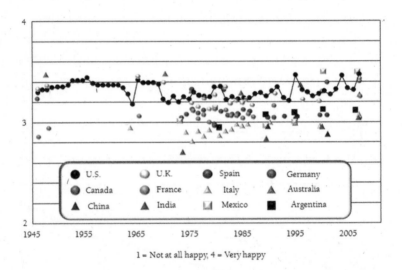

1 = Not at all happy; 4 = Very happy

Source: Internet Appendix to Inglehart, Foa, and Welzel, "Social Change, Freedom and Rising Happiness," *Journal of Personality and Social Psychology*

The problem is that although poverty definitely brings about misery, money cannot buy happiness. Economist Richard Easterlin's seminal work on the relationship between prosperity and happiness showed that once a country was no longer poor, greater wealth did not make its people happier.

Is there any group more likely to be happy? The answer is *yes*. But some of the groups cited might surprise you: the American Amish, the Greenlandic Inughuit, and the Kenyan Maasai, all people who lead materially simple lives and live in cultures that are very different from most of society.

In fact, the Amish are frequently shown to be "imperturbably sunny." Why is that? Sociology professor Donald Kraybill observes, "The roots of their happiness are tied to their communal values. They talk about cooperation. They talk about self-denial. They talk about giving up things for the sake of the community." To quote one woman from the Amish community, "You have lots of cousins, maybe 100 or 150, that would always be there to take care of you if you have a need. It's a security we probably take for granted."

In many parts of the world, "extended" families represent the core family structure. In addition to parents and their children, grandparents, aunts, uncles, and cousins serve as a tight-knit community. Western societies, however, have tended to gravitate toward "nuclear" families, with a mom, dad, and children. As a result, the extended family-based communities of many cultures tend to be truncated to immediate families in the West.

But even the nuclear family is no longer an adequate reflection of the typical family in the West. In 1950, 45 percent of families could be classified as nuclear—today, that number is less than 25 percent. The reasons for this are numerous—an aging population, increasing divorce rates, increasing numbers of people who never marry, etc.—but the result is a society increasingly disconnected from the family-based community structures of our past.

This shift in family structure is occurring as our societies are becoming increasingly urban. This is not surprising. Typically, cities offer a greater diversity of economic and cultural opportunities. Therefore, in our pursuit of happiness, it is only natural that more of us would gravitate toward them.

The increase in urbanization, however, decreases social interaction. Ironically, while we are living in societies with increasing numbers of people in close proximity to one another, urbanization actually discourages interconnectedness.

The problem is, as psychologist David Myers observes, "Close, supportive, connected relationships make for happiness, and we have fewer of those relationships today." As a result, too often we find that we are not happy because we have neglected the foundation for happiness in our pursuit of it.

Frittered Away

What ails us is not the result of what we naturally lack. Rather, it is the result of what we willingly barter away. We are exchanging loyalties in our pursuit of happiness without realizing that by trading away our loyalties we actually erode the foundation of our happiness.

The economic engine that has saved us from the yoke of poverty has also taught us to trade our time and labor to get the things that we want. The problem isn't that we are exchanging our time for commodities, but instead we are exchanging our family's time, our friends' time, our ideals' time to get some*thing*.

Of course, there is nothing wrong with buying things. And there is nothing wrong with sacrificing to get the things we want. The problem is that we do a terrible job of predicting what will actually make us happy, so we make very bad decisions regarding what we are willing to sacrifice versus what we hope to obtain.

Study after study shows that we take far more pleasure in experiences than in things. Why? Because experiences— a good meal, vacations, movies, etc.—tend to be events we share with other people, whereas objects typically are not. This is not surprising given that the most important factor that separates happy people from unhappy people is our relationships with others. It is more important than money, and even more important than our health. Yet we frequently trade our loyalties for things that will not make us happier, namely money.

To quote Harvard professor Daniel Gilbert, perhaps the world's leading authority on happiness, "What I've learned from data is that I don't chase dollars now that I have enough of them, because I know that it will take a very large amount of money to increase my happiness by a small amount. You couldn't pay me $100,000 to miss a play date with my granddaughters. And that's not because I'm rich. That's because I know that a hundred grand won't make me as happy as nurturing my relationship with my granddaughters will."

Treatment

Our loyalties encompass every aspect of our lives: our personal, economic, spiritual, and societal relationships. The repercussions of our loyalties impact not just our *everyday* world but *the* world. So curing what ails our world begins with curing what ails us.

The first step in healing our loyalty sickness begins with introspection. We need to make a candid appraisal of ourselves, to understand how we connect with others.

We also must ask ourselves honest questions about the role that loyalty plays in all aspects of our lives. If we do this, we will almost certainly see where we can improve the quality of our lives and add to the happiness of others and ourselves at the same time. LoyaltyAdvisor will provide an in-depth survey, but for now, take a minute to consider the following questions. They provide a starting point in assessing our loyalty strengths and weaknesses. On a scale of 1–5, with 1 = completely disagree and 5 = completely agree, how would you respond to each of the following statements?

1. I never sacrifice relationships with my family, friends, and loved ones because of my career.	1 2 3 4 5
2. I never feel jealous of my friends' successes.	1 2 3 4 5
3. I give unconditionally, expecting nothing in return, in my relationships with family, friends, and loved ones.	1 2 3 4 5
4. When deciding where I spend my money, I always choose positive relationships over price.	1 2 3 4 5
5. I consciously make the effort every week to spend time with those to whom I owe loyalty.	1 2 3 4 5
6. I always keep both the implicit and explicit commitments I make.	1 2 3 4 5
7. I am strongly loyal to my current employer.	1 2 3 4 5
8. I have made significant sacrifices to carry out my commitments to my friends, family, and loved ones over the past twelve months.	1 2 3 4 5
9. My friends would say without reservation that I am "fiercely loyal" to them.	1 2 3 4 5

If you answered "5" to each of these questions, you are either the reincarnation of Mother Teresa or you are kidding yourself. In any case, there are no right answers; the point is to start truly thinking about the role loyalty plays in your life. These self-assessment questions are intended to awaken you to the opportunity that you have to make loyalty a bigger part of your life.

Fulfillment

How can I be fulfilled? We all yearn for the answer to this question. Yet we dedicate very little of our lives actually trying to uncover it.

Instead, we do *things* designed to make us feel significant, stimulated, and secure. We spend our time pursuing wealth, power, fame, excellence, or knowledge. Nothing is inherently wrong with this. But accomplishing these goals never results in a sustained sense of well-being.

Fulfillment only comes when we give of ourselves to others. Loyalty, like love, is not something you get but something you give. But, like love, giving loyalty, over time, through difficulties and trials, leads to mutual loyalty. And it leads to relationships that are a profound source of satisfaction and happiness that cannot be built any other way.

Harvard professor of philosophy Josiah Royce observed almost a century ago that loyalty is what each of us is seeking and that we can "find spiritual rest and peace in nothing else." It binds us together—family, friend, and lover—through good times and bad. And for society as a whole, it is the means by which principles reign over self-interest.

We have choices in everything we do. We can change the way things *will be*. We can build loyal relationships that lift us up in all aspects of our lives—relationships that keep us fulfilled and happy.

But this doesn't just happen. It requires that we question some of our current beliefs, and change some of our long-standing behaviors.

So, are you up to the challenge? If yes, then read on.

Chapter 2

Know Yourself

Self-knowledge is the beginning of self-improvement.

—Baltasar Gracián (1601–1658),
Spanish author

"I'm good enough. I'm smart enough. And doggone it, people like me!" Often, our introspective self-examinations more closely resemble the television comedy skit "Daily Affirmations with Stuart Smalley" from *Saturday Night Live* than a realistic appraisal.

Anyone who has ever spent an evening at an "Open Mic Night" or watched the auditions for *American Idol* quickly realizes that few of the wannabe Tim McGraws and Faith Hills actually have the talent for the job. Yet frequently the negative reaction of the audience (or Simon Cowell) is summarily dismissed by the singers instead of taken as an accurate assessment of their abilities.

While we may find such self-delusion humorous, pitiable, or frustrating, the fact is that we all lack objectivity when evaluating ourselves. We tend to minimize our failings and overstate our strengths, and to hold on to information that supports our view and forget conflicting facts. This is how our brains work—they try to reconcile our self-image with our interactions with our environment.

Challenges to our self-image make us uncomfortable. As renowned author Aldous Huxley observed, "If most of us remain ignorant of ourselves, it is because self-knowledge is painful and we prefer the pleasures of illusion."

Improving our connections with others invariably begins with improving ourselves. But without a realistic assessment of who we are, we are flying blind. We need to know how we interact with others. We need to be clear as to where our loyalties really lie. And we need to know what this has to do with our being happy.

LoyaltyAdvisor

Most of us are loyal to something other than ourselves, but to unlock the power of loyalty in our lives, we need clarity regarding "how loyal" we really are, and "to what" we are especially loyal.

Theoretically, if we were completely objective, we could take time and write down all of the things to which we are loyal. We could then group these loyalties into different categories. Finally, we could assign a rating to identify the strength of our loyalties for each of these categories.

Most of us, however, do not have the time or the impartiality to do this type of self-analysis. Moreover, even if we did, we would have no idea how our loyalties relate to who we are in terms of how we connect with others and to our ultimate happiness.

To help provide this insight, this book includes free one-time access to LoyaltyAdvisor, a revolutionary tool for examining our loyalties. LoyaltyAdvisor provides an assessment of our relationship styles and an examination of our loyalties across multiple areas that have been proven to correlate to our happiness.

The various relationship styles, and what they mean, are described later in this chapter.

LoyaltyAdvisor also allows us to benchmark our relationship styles and loyalty levels vis-à-vis the top 15 percent of individuals in life satisfaction. The purpose of benchmarking is not to suggest that we change who we naturally are. Rather, it is to help us recognize aspects of our relationship styles and loyalties that have the potential to impact our happiness either positively or negatively. All dimensions of our relationship style have pros and cons. It is up to us to recognize and act on the potential negative aspects while maintaining the strength associated with each dimension. The benchmark serves to highlight which areas are more likely to play a role in our happiness.

Taking LoyaltyAdvisor

To take the LoyaltyAdvisor assessment, you must first log onto the Internet and go to the following URL: http://www. loyaltyadvisor.com. You will be prompted to provide a unique access code, which is located on the reverse side of the dust jacket of this book.

You will first be asked some questions about yourself (and your work, if applicable). You will then be taken through a series of questions designed to identify your relationship style and loyalty levels. This will take about fifteen minutes to complete and must be completed in one uninterrupted session. Immediately after you complete LoyaltyAdvisor, a copy of your assessment report will be emailed to you.

In addition, LoyaltyAdvisor provides you with the opportunity to have your friends and family assess your loyalty to them. Because the perceptions of our family and friends are likely to differ from our own, we strongly encourage you to take advantage of this opportunity to see yourself through the eyes of others.

LoyaltyAdvisor allows for up to ten of your friends and family members to provide feedback. In order to protect the anonymity of the respondents, at least three email addresses are required to gain access to the friends/family assessment, and there must be at least three respondents for you to view their ratings of you. Therefore, before you begin LoyaltyAdvisor, you should have available the email addresses of those individuals from whom you would like to gather opinions. One week after completing Loyalty-Advisor and inputting these email addresses, you will be emailed a copy of your LoyaltyAdvisor Friends & Family assessment report.

Remember that the purpose of LoyaltyAdvisor is to provide insight into ourselves. It is not designed to make claims regarding whether or not we are loyal. Rather, it helps us to understand how we present ourselves to others, to see where our loyalties lie, and to identify where this may impact our ultimate happiness. Furthermore, for those of us who choose to get feedback from our friends and family—highly recommended—LoyaltyAdvisor provides invaluable insight into the differences between how we perceive our loyalty and how those to whom we owe loyalty perceive us.

How Do I Relate?

> I am currently watching [the British television show] *Richard & Judy*, and Richard is gradually winding me up. He constantly belittles Judy, interrupts her when she is speaking, asks the guests questions and then answers for them, and thinks he is so funny! Is it just me or do other people feel the same? [Posted on Yahoo! Answers]

Whether or not we have ever seen the *Richard & Judy* television show, all of us—whether we agree or not—can connect with how she feels. Why? Because all of us have felt similarly about someone we've known. And, truth be told, someone has most likely felt similarly about us.

At some level, we probably recognize that something about us contributed to the discord. But more often than not, most of us tend to think something to the effect of "What's wrong with him?" Assuming that nothing is really *wrong* with either of us, then most likely our relationship styles were incompatible.

Each of us has our own *Relationship DNA* that serves as the code for how we interact with one another. While no two people are identical in how they connect with others, our research finds that we are all made up of the same ten basic building blocks:

- Leadership
- Reliance
- Empathy
- Security
- Calculativeness
- Connectedness
- Independence
- Traditionalism
- Problem-Focused Coping
- Emotion-Focused Coping

Being high or low on a particular factor does not imply good or bad, as each factor has the potential to have both a positive and negative impact on our relationships, regardless of where we fall on the factor. For example, being high in Reliance (i.e., our ability to trust and attach to people) makes it relatively easy to include others in our lives but also has the potential to cause us to see others as "crutches" rather than a social support network. On the other hand, being low in Reliance makes it much easier for us to solve problems on our own but also has the potential to lessen our ability to recognize and seek help from others when we really need it.

Some of these factors will be more prominent in our lives than others, but all will have an impact on how we interact to some degree. And while there will be others who possess a relationship style that's similar to ours, no one is exactly like us. In fact, we are able to build strong, loyal relationships with one another precisely because each of us is different. It is our differences that allow us to enrich one another's lives.

We all have differing relationship styles.

Source: Ipsos Loyalty

The Components of Our Relationship Style

LEADERSHIP

Leadership describes your belief in your ability to occupy a leadership position effectively and to influence others to follow you voluntarily. It describes to what extent you view yourself as a leader. The qualities that make a leader are encased within a general sense of being in control of yourself and your surroundings, being motivated to achieve success, attaining a comfort level interacting with others, and not being afraid to take risks.

If you are an individual high in Leadership, you may find that . . . A leader's competitive spirit fuels ambition, and people see this fortitude and are happy to follow it. Although these characteristics help you understand how to engage others and get them on board, it has the potential to alienate people around you as others may view you as being too competitive and aggressive.

If you are an individual low in Leadership, you may find that . . . While a less competitive and aggressive attitude may make people around you feel comfortable, it may hinder your ability to engage with others successfully and get them onboard.

RELIANCE

Reliance describes how well you come to trust and attach to people around you. It illustrates the desire to have a personal support web that is founded on openness and accountability. Reliance entails opening up to others quickly, readily, and with little difficulty. It is typified by a willingness to ask for help when it's needed.

If you are an individual high in Reliance, you may find that . . .
Opening up to others is a relatively easy task and you are happy to include people in your life. Your perseverance and your desire for trust ensures that many of the acquaintances or friends you have are long term. Stretching yourself, however, to rely on others can make you vulnerable, bringing with it the risk of disappointment in others. It also has the potential to dampen confidence in your ability to overcome problems on your own and can lead you to see others as a crutch rather than a social support network.

If you are an individual low in Reliance, you may find that . . .
You tend to solve problems autonomously without depending on others. Although protecting yourself from being overly reliant on others lessens your vulnerability to being disappointed in others, the limits you impose on your perseverance and trust in others have the potential to hamper your ability to build long-term relationships.

EMPATHY

Empathy describes how well you are able to identify and sympathize with others. It is the tendency to adopt a more flexible outlook and to accept and appreciate people for who they are. This brings with it warmth and friendliness that is inviting to others.

If you are an individual high in Empathy, you may find that . . .
You tend to approach others in a compassionate, kind-hearted, and understanding way. You can see problems through the eyes and hearts of others, and this wins you admiration and affection, whether you know it or not. There may be times, however, when your empathetic nature can burden you and make you feel that others inadvertently take advantage of you by consistently seeking you out for help or advice.

If you are an individual low in Empathy, you may find that . . .
You tend to avoid finding yourself in situations where you feel burdened by other people's problems. As a result, you are less at risk of being taken advantage of. But this can also prevent you from seeing problems through the eyes and hearts of others, which has the potential to create distance between yourself and others.

SECURITY

Security describes a general sense of stability and comfort with yourself and your environment. It endorses a feeling that things are going well and there is no need to worry excessively or be anxious. This leads to a life with a lower amount of stress and pressure, ultimately weeding out being needlessly encumbered by a sense of the impending.

If you are an individual high in Security, you may find that . . .
You have a sense of reassurance and comfort and are able to enjoy the moment. You are relaxed and are able to manage anxiety and stress successfully. An overly relaxed attitude, however, may get in the way of your ability to foresee situations and be preemptive about sources of risk that have the potential to cause problems in the future.

If you are an individual low in Security, you may find that . . .
You are more likely to feel on edge, to have an underlying sense that something is wrong or that things are going to go wrong. And although this prevents you from getting too comfortable, it also results in greater worries, which has the potential to impact your ability to enjoy the moment.

CALCULATIVENESS

Calculativeness describes your ability to control and promote your image and ideal environment for your personal benefit.

It is an ongoing evaluation of others and the role they play in your life based on the innate belief that there are multiple layers to every person and every interaction. This brings with it a level of formality in interactions and selective articulation of yourself, and control over self-presentation.

If you are an individual high in Calculativeness, you may find that . . .
You are able to surmise the potential gains and losses for you in a relationship. You place importance on showcasing yourself in the right way. This has the potential, however, to cause others to view you as less sincere and less worthy of their complete trust. It may also lead others to perceive you as being unemotional and manipulative in some circumstances.

If you are an individual low in Calculativeness, you may find that . . .
You are less likely to see relationships as a means of potential gains versus potential losses. You are also more comfortable being yourself instead of controlling how your image is showcased. This can lead others to view you as more sincere and worthy of their trust. Although the ability to be yourself is reassuring, it has the potential to bring with it a sense that you are being too naïve and not realizing the full potential of opportunities that present themselves.

CONNECTEDNESS

Connectedness describes how you view and interact with others on a personal level. Close and tight relationships typify the crux of this dimension. A feeling of connection to others forms the basis and bedrock of happiness. It encompasses a style of frequent and close interaction and navigating people and drawing them close with ease.

If you are an individual high in Connectedness, you may find that . . .
You tend to be passionate about the relationships in your life and you invest time, effort, and faith in developing them. When a relationship begins to fail, however, it results in restlessness. Because of the value placed on personal connections with others, it can become uncomfortable if a connection deteriorates.

If you are an individual low in Connectedness, you may find that . . .
Given that less of your happiness hinges on the closeness of the relationships you have, there is less room for disappointment and discomfort when a personal connection deteriorates. This has the potential, however, to cause you to feel like a loner or to lead to a life of primarily casual friendships/relationships that lack the fulfillment that deep and intense bonds provide.

INDEPENDENCE

Independence describes the level of comfort with spending time by yourself or leading an autonomous life. It is about your approach to feeling control over your own destiny. Self-discipline and thoroughness are all integral components of this outlook.

If you are an individual high in Independence, you may find that . . .
You tend to feel like you're in the driver's seat. You tend to have strong self-discipline, but you can get disappointed in yourself when this discipline breaks down. Your independence reduces your chances of getting disappointed by others, but you have the potential to be missing out on valuable opportunities to capitalize on other people's ideas and strengths.

If you are an individual low in Independence, you may find that . . .
Your reduced sense of independence allows you to take advantage of and capitalize on other people's ideas. You are more likely to take pleasure in the company of others. These tendencies, however, have the potential to lead you to over-rely on others, missing out on the opportunity to make decisions that would best suit your needs.

TRADITIONALISM

Traditionalism describes your perceptions on the nature and pace of your preferred everyday life. It reflects the desire for consistency, normalcy, and regularity. It brings with it a sense of caution when approaching truly unfamiliar situations, and a tendency to operate within your comfort zone. There is no felt need to show off or flaunt.

If you are an individual high in Traditionalism, you may find that . . .
You tend to prefer to take the safe route, the tried-and-true way of getting things done. You also are cautious in new environments. You don't flaunt your success, instead preferring humility. As a result, however, others may remain in the dark about your achievements and potential, and you may be missing out on new experiences that could potentially provide you with novel perspectives and excitement.

If you are an individual low in Traditionalism, you may find that . . .
You are more likely to be open to new ideas and experiences. This enables you to take advantage of different and novel perspectives. You tend to be more accepting of change and of getting out of your comfort zone. As a result of these tendencies, however, you have the potential to get sidetracked or feel like you are lost in unchartered territory.

PROBLEM-FOCUSED COPING

Problem-focused coping refers to how you go about meeting challenges, overcoming obstacles, making choices and withstanding the consequences of those decisions. Problem-focused coping describes a planned and rational approach to solving problems, where negative emotions are avoided by taking some action to modify, avoid, or minimize the threatening situation.

If you are an individual high in Problem-Focused Coping, you may find that . . .
You employ a strong sense of reason and rationality when addressing a problem. You like to examine the problem from multiple angles so that you get a feel for the issue at hand and create a mental plan for dismantling each issue you encounter. This tendency has the potential, however, to get you caught up in presenting your case in a matter-of-fact way, which can at times make you appear cold or callous to others.

If you are an individual low in Problem-Focused Coping, you may find that . . .
You are less likely to address problems using a methodical, analytic framework. This tendency, however, could hinder you from identifying and effectively addressing the root cause of a problem.

EMOTION-FOCUSED COPING

Emotion-focused coping refers to how you go about meeting challenges, overcoming obstacles, making choices, and withstanding the consequences of those decisions. Emotion-focused coping describes an approach that focuses on managing one's emotions in solving problems and unpleasant emotions are directly moderated or eliminated.

If you are an individual high in Emotion-Focused Coping, you may find that . . .
You tend to display your emotions openly and seek out advice and comfort from others. At times when confronted with problems, you would prefer to focus on something other than the issue that is bothering you. While this tendency allows you to keep your emotions under control, it has the potential to make you overly focused on the emotions you experience and less focused on addressing the problem at hand.

If you are an individual low in Emotion-Focused Coping, you may find that . . .
You tend to be less likely to display your emotions and to seek out advice and comfort from others when confronted with a problem. Rather, your tendency is to focus on what is bothering you. This tendency may help you focus on solving the problem at hand, but it may also cause you to suppress

your feelings, and miss out on getting valuable advice from others.

Loyalty Bonds Different Relationship Styles

Virtually all of us can think of someone in our lives with whom we interact positively but who also has traits that annoy us. Our friends can at times say the same about us.

All of us have aspects to our relationship styles that make us less than attractive at times to people who are very important to us. Even the most narcissistic among us inherently recognizes this to be true. Still, we make the effort to hold on to these connections. Why?

Our loyalties to one another mediate the connection between our differing relationship styles. Were this not the case, at some point all of our relationships would disintegrate.

And we cherish this aspect of loyalty. It means that we won't be abandoned when we aren't on our best behavior.

In fact, sometimes we stay in a relationship merely because of that person's loyalty to us. It's why we often hear something equivalent to "He may be deeply flawed, but *at least he is loyal.*" For example, it isn't difficult to find quotes like this sprinkled throughout the Internet:

- "He may be worthless, but at least he is loyal."
- "Granted [he] has not done a bang-up job either, but at least he is loyal to those around him."

- "She might be a b@#*!, but at least she is loyal to her friends."

For loyalty to mediate our different relationship styles, however, it is not enough simply to feel loyal. The object of our loyalty (friends, family, etc.) must perceive that we have acted and will continue to act with loyalty toward them. Often, however, this is where things break down—our perceptions of our loyalty often differ considerably from those of our friends and family.

Self-Discovery

We all want to be happy. It is in our nature to prefer to bask in the warmth of positive feedback. It is also natural to fear information that challenges our self-image.

This puts us in a catch-22. Being happy requires that we confront the things that keep us from getting there. And what keeps us from getting there often exists inside of us—in particular, in how we live our loyalties.

The place to begin is to know where you are. We need to know how we define our loyalties. But, as an old saying goes, "You can't see the picture when you're inside the frame." So we need to know how we present our loyalties to others.

We hope that by revealing your loyalties—both from your perspective and the perspective of your friends and family—that you can identify not only where you are but the direction you need to go to get you where you want to be. Our loyalties define who we are. By understanding and acting on them, we can define who we will become.

＊ ＊ ＊

This is a good time to visit http://www.loyaltyadvisor.com and complete the self-assessment, including supplying the email addresses of people who you would like to contribute to your assessment by providing you with an independent and confidential assessment of their perceptions of your loyalty. In chapter nine, we'll provide some guidance on what to do next in your loyalty journey.

Chapter 3

Building Loyal Relationships

Nobody would choose to live without friends, even if he had all other good things.

—Aristotle

When most of us think of our strongest loyalties, we tend to think of friends, family, spouses, and lovers. In fact, for most of us, these loyalties have the greatest influence on our happiness.

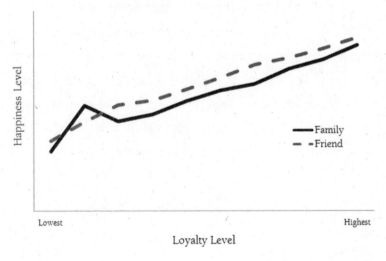

Happiness Level by Loyalty Level

Source: Ipsos Loyalty

Sadly, research today indicates that the number and quality of friendships for the average American has been declining since at least 1985. In fact, 25 percent of Americans report having no close friends in whom they could confide things that were important to them. And the average total number of confidants per person is only two. Just twenty years ago—within our very own lifetimes—the average American had three people with whom he/she could share important issues. The depressing truth is that an estimated 10 to 15 percent of the U.S. population are chronically lonely—this is somewhere between 30 and 45 million people!

And we aren't only watching the number and quality of our friendships decline. Marriages today are far more likely to end in divorce than they were fifty years ago. And at the other extreme, the percentage of individuals who never marry has also risen dramatically—in some countries precipitously. For example, in Japan, the rise in the number of people choosing to forgo marriage has led to a declining birth rate and an aging population that, if left unchecked, will make it impossible to sustain its economy.

Marriage and Divorce Statistics for the United States

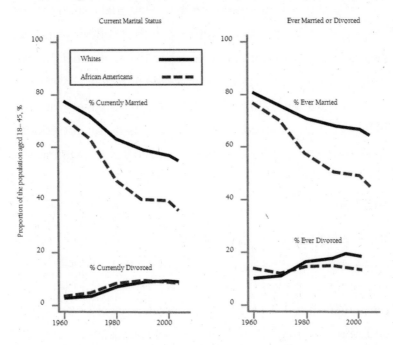

Source: Betsey Stevenson and Justin Wolfers (2007), "Marriage and Divorce: Changes and Their Driving Forces," *Journal of Economic Perspectives,* vol. 21, no. 2 (Spring), page 36.

Interestingly, it's not that we lack information designed to help us in making our relationships work. In fact, a quick check of Books in Print reveals that this is an extremely important topic to us. Almost fifty thousand books have been written on making friends alone. And many, if not most, of the more than one hundred thousand books on relationships (friendship, marriage, etc.) offer valuable insight.

So why the disconnect? Why in the age of information are we unable to build relationships that make us happier? Clearly, the time pressures of living in the modern world eat away at our opportunities to connect with one another. But we believe that this is not the root cause of the problem. Rather, it is our unwillingness to see our own role in the general decline of loyalty that is a major cause of relationship disintegration. And this disintegration ultimately leads to our unhappiness.

Sticking

If you ask a four-year-old what a friend is, she is likely to give a response regarding someone who happens to be near her or whose toys she likes. A five- or-six-year-old would focus on particular episodes where they interact. At ages seven, eight, and nine, children begin to realize that friendship is personal, and they may like or dislike a person due to some trait.

In later years, however, we begin to realize that human relationships are complex. When adults are asked what friendship means, some of the most frequent words that come forth are *loyalty, honesty, respect, trust, intimacy, help,* and *support*. This is true across cultures.

So why do we build strong relationships with some and not others? Part of the reason is that we naturally gravitate to people like ourselves. We tend to be more comfortable with people who have relationship styles similar to our own. The more alike our interests and attitudes are, the more likely we are to be friends.

Common interests make us more likeable to each other. And we all like to be liked! Not surprisingly, we tend to like people who like us and dislike people who do not like us.

But our commonalities will only take us so far. Strong relationships (be they friends, family, lovers, etc.) create an implied promise: *I will be there for you!* It is this loyalty that differentiates friend from acquaintance, companion from escort.

Loyalty at its essence is about sticking with one another. It means that we strongly intend to keep the relationship going. It means that we are emotionally attached to one another. And it means that we envision a future together.

The loyal are not simply members of the entourage that inevitably arrives when things are going well. It's easy to get people to come to the party. But when the party's over, who is there to help you clean up? Any fan of American blues music will recall the familiar lament of the famed Lonnie Johnson: "When I had plenty of money, I had friends all over town, but just as soon as I got outdoors, none of my friends could be found." As Oprah Winfrey notes, "Lots of people want to ride with you in the limo, but what you want is someone who will take the bus with you when the limo breaks down."

Loyal companions can rely on one another. This interdependence actually affects our motives, preferences, behaviors, and outcomes. In healthy relationships, it helps us to become better people than we could be alone. But it requires forgoing our immediate self-interest to help a friend in need. In other words, loyalty at times demands sacrifice.

It is the testing of bonds in difficult times because of loyalty that is the hallmark of strong relationships. Knowing that someone will be there for us when the going gets tough provides us with immense security. And it is virtually impossible to be happy until we feel secure.

Forgiveness

"I'm only human." We all say it. But we don't say it to indicate that we are the most advanced life form currently proven to exist in the universe. We say it to indicate that there will be times when we will disappoint others . . . and ourselves.

Nowhere are we more human than in our relationships with others. We are rarely more emotionally vulnerable. And as we envision the future of our closest relationships, we can be certain of one thing—at some point everyone who is close to us will disappoint us so long as we both live long enough. This means that at some point, we too will disappoint those for whom we care most deeply.

These experiences hurt—especially those failures that we believe are particularly disloyal. Even today, it is easy for the authors to remember the hurt felt as a child at having our secrets shared openly with others by friends. And the scars never seem to heal fully when recalling the pain of having let down a friend.

Yes, this is indeed part of being human. It is so much of who we are that all major religious faiths address the fact that we will at times fall short of our duty of loyalty.

A particularly poignant story in the New Testament tells of Peter, one of the twelve apostles and one of the first disciples of Jesus. Peter is portrayed throughout the New Testament as the most loyal follower of Jesus and his role in the early Christian church is beyond dispute. Many Christian followers believe Peter was the first bishop of Rome and a martyr under Nero, and that he was crucified upside down because he believed himself unworthy to die in the same manner as Jesus.

Despite this ardent faith, however, all the Gospels in the New Testament detail that Jesus foretold to Peter that he would renounce his association with Him three times that very night. Peter protested strongly, vowing, "I will not deny you." But after Jesus was arrested by the Romans, Peter did exactly as Jesus had predicted. At sunrise, Peter, overcome with remorse at his disloyalty, broke down weeping.

Even the most loyal relationships are open and vulnerable to potential betrayal, conflict, and negative outcomes. This can easily lead us to become jaded about relationships and approach new experiences with our guard up. While this makes perfect sense from a survival instinct perspective, it causes us to miss out on rewarding experiences we could have had with others.

Although a certain degree of caution is critical to emotional survival, being overly cautious is extremely detrimental. It leads us to form prejudices against potential new relationships even when it is not warranted. While there may be some truth to the saying "good fences make good neighbors," a wall with no gates in it is a prison. As poet Robert Frost writes in the poem "Mending Wall":

> Before I built a wall I'd ask to know,
> What I was walling in or walling out.

Frost beautifully captures the paradox in human nature. We want a wall to protect ourselves from being hurt by others, but walls also keep friends out.

The story of Peter serves to remind us that all of us are indeed human. In the end, our ability to hold onto our relationships lies in our power to forgive—to forgo a desire for retribution and a demand for atonement.

As British poet Alexander Pope observed, "To err is human, to forgive divine." The truth is that we all fail. Promises sometimes get broken. But loyalty to our relationships requires that we make the best effort to understand the conflict and deal with it in the best possible way. And when we fail, we must make every effort to restore what we have damaged.

Perception Is Reality

For those of us who took advantage of the opportunity in LoyaltyAdvisor to have friends and family members assess our loyalty, the results consistently point to areas where we can do a better job of expressing our loyalty to them. Often, the results reveal a great divide between how we view our loyalty and how our friends and family view it.

Do our friends believe without a doubt that we convincingly demonstrate our loyalty to them? Are they certain that we have and will continue to . . .

- Devote enough time to our relationships with them?
- Stand up for them when it is uncomfortable, even risky, to do so?
- Celebrate their successes without envy?
- Support them during difficult times?
- Hold fast to information provided in confidence?
- Make every effort to carry our commitments to them even when it requires considerable self-sacrifice?

This isn't easy to do. In some aspect of our relationships, virtually all of us disappoint in conveying our loyalty to friends and family. We all know this. Yet somehow knowing this intellectually doesn't make it less uncomfortable to have it confirmed.

So instead of really listening for constructive feedback to guide us in improving our relationships with those who mean the most to our happiness, we typically seek confirmation that everything is okay. But improvement never comes with being satisfied with where you are.

Developing loyal lifelong relationships requires that we demonstrate that we deserve such loyalty. We must listen to what our friends and companions want and need, help them achieve their goals when we can, and be considerate, kind, and supportive in good times and bad. While this sounds obvious, most of us do not spend enough time actually doing this.

And perhaps most important, *be thankful* for great, loyal friends and companions. Show them that you appreciate them! Psychologists have conclusively proven that expressing appreciation on a regular basis is associated with a more fulfilling and meaningful life.

If we make this a way of life, great things are sure to happen. We will develop lasting loyal friendships. We will be happier! Loyal friends and companions pour themselves into us, just as we pour ourselves into them. As a result, we are filled to overflowing!

But oh! the blessing it is to have a friend to whom one can speak fearlessly on any subject; with whom one's deepest as well as most foolish thoughts come out simply and safely. Oh, the comfort—the inexpressible comfort of feeling safe with a person—having neither to weigh thoughts nor measure words, but pouring them all right out, just as they are, chaff and grain together; certain that a faithful hand will take and sift them, keep what is worth keeping, and then with the breath of kindness blow the rest away.

—Dinah Maria Craik, *A Life for a Life* (1859)

Chapter 4

The Economics of Loyalty

Our better product is more than just the DIRECTV and XM radio we're getting on and the Fox movies we are putting on. What you can't buy is the loyalty that comes through our dedicated crewmembers.

—David Neeleman, founder and former CEO
of JetBlue Airways

Nothing will take up more of our time as adults than work—not family time, recreation, eating, or even sleeping. Whether we like it or not, the overwhelming majority of us do not have the luxury of opting out of work, given our need for food, clothing, and shelter. And, put in the terms of a courtroom drama, for most of us work is a fifty-year sentence (from approximately age twenty to age seventy) with typically 80 percent of time served before becoming eligible for early release (i.e., retirement). This, of course, assumes that we actually live long enough to fulfill our sentence—hardly a certainty.

Obviously, work is critical to our survival, and its role in our lives is pervasive. Most of us would find life extremely harsh without a job. Despite the obligatory nature of work for most of us, however, work actually helps shape our identity and provides us with social connections. It also strongly influences our psychological health. If we are happy at work, we are much more likely to be happy in general, and vice versa. And dissatisfaction at work often leads to a host of problems, including anxiety and depression, which impacts far more than our employment.

Percent of Day Spent Unhappy by Level of Job Satisfaction

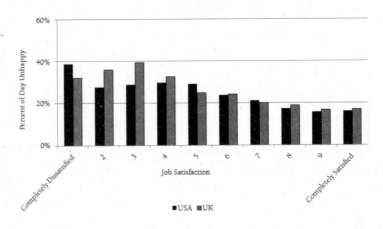

Source: Ipsos Loyalty

Most of us at some level recognize the importance of our work to our sense of security and how we view ourselves. And virtually all of us sense a decline in company–employee loyalty in comparison with our parents' and grandparents' generations. It is readily apparent in the rise in job-hopping for us as workers, and the increased willingness to down-size by companies.

But what most of us fail to see is how the shift in loyalty in our work environment has changed how we see the world and our place in it. Because our economic success is increasingly dependent upon our ability to retool our skills and reboot our careers, we are often forced to exchange one work relationship for another to stay current and relevant in an ever-changing, intensely competitive marketplace. And we are sometimes even required to relocate to maintain employment. This makes it difficult to sustain our bonds with one another.

Of course, constant change is the nature of capitalism. Competition ensures that more innovative firms grow at the expense of established companies—a process that economist Joseph Schumpeter called "creative destruction." But the speed with which this destruction of established institutions now happens is unprecedented.

For us as individuals, constant economic change means that we feel always on the brink of losing control. We are forced to live in the moment, and leave tomorrow for the future. What this teaches us can be summed up in the phrase, "What have you done for me lately?"

This is the antithesis of loyalty. Loyalty requires a commitment to the future. As noted London School of Economics and New York University professor Richard Sennett observes, "'No long term' is a principle which corrodes trust, loyalty, and mutual commitment ... social bonds take time to develop, slowly rooting into the cracks and crevices of institutions."

Clearly, the decline in loyalty is not good for us as individuals. But what most managers do not realize is that this is absolutely terrible for companies as well!

Loyalty is the *right* strategy in all aspects of our economic lives: as employees, as customers, as managers, and as business owners. And by *right*, we mean that it tangibly maximizes value—emotional *and* economic.

So this raises a question: If a loyalty strategy maximizes profits, and capitalism is about business success, why isn't loyalty the predominant strategy? Well, it's the classic "prisoner's dilemma" problem. If everybody is out for themselves, we end up worse off than if we cooperate with one another. And we choose not to cooperate because we don't understand why it is in our interest to do so.

Maximizing value through loyalty requires that we know how to do it, and what the upside is. Fortunately, we can and will do exactly that. We will show why employee and customer loyalty matter for companies. We will also show why our loyalty as employees and customers actually matters to us.

The Why of Employee Loyalty for Companies

The greater the loyalty of a group toward the group, the greater is the motivation among the members to achieve the goals of the group, and the greater the probability that the group will achieve its goals.

—Rensis Likert (1903–1981), educator and organizational psychologist

(This section of the chapter focuses on why managers should care about employee and customer loyalty. Readers not interested in customer and employee management may wish to skip ahead to the section of this chapter titled *The Why of Employee Loyalty for Me.*)

The long-term success of any company depends heavily upon the quality and loyalty of its people. Few corporate executives would disagree with this idea conceptually. But it is also true that most treat the economic value of employees in enhancing customer relationships and company profits as "soft" numbers, unlike the "hard" numbers they use to manage their operations, like the cost of labor.

The problem with this is that when the going gets tough, managers focus on the hard numbers. And the reality is that at some point every company will go through tough times. That is the nature of the cycles of business.

The result is that today we are overwhelmed with downsizings and restructurings. Layoffs make the front pages of our newspapers regularly. And while Wall Street often rewards layoffs by treating them as a sign that management is serious about getting a company's financial house in order, the reality is quite different. Most organizations that downsize fail to realize any long-term cost savings or efficiencies, which necessitates more restructurings and layoffs.

Although the cost benefits tend to be mirages, the corresponding pain to customers and employees is all too real. Research using the American Customer Satisfaction Index found that those firms that engaged in substantial downsizing experienced large declines in customer satisfaction. Unfortunately for those firms, the index has proven to be a good predictor of future earnings. The study's authors note that "the current trend toward downsizing in U.S. firms may increase productivity in the short term, but the downsized firms' future financial performance will suffer if repeat business is dependent on labor-intensive customized service."

The impact on the organization's culture is also severe. Downsizings result in rumor-fueled paranoia. When Coca-Cola instituted a restructuring that resulted in the loss of thousands of jobs, the company became so awash in far-fetched stories that executives were forced to take the unusual step of intervening to quash them.

Worse still, employees that remain often find themselves jaded. It isn't hard to find employees who feel exactly like Dan after his company's layoffs in Mitchell Lee Marks's *Charging Back Up the Hill*:

> There is no loyalty here; no one is going the extra mile after this. Two years ago, we worked sixty-five-hour weeks. People were willing to do it, because it was a great place to work and we were doing something that mattered. . . . From here on in, it's just a job for me. I'll put in my forty hours and that's it.

Let's be clear. No CEO relishes the thought of layoffs. It means that their companies are floundering. Furthermore, history has shown us that the pain often outweighs any long-term financial gains.

If companies are going to grow their way out of difficult times (and excel in good times), they need two things: 1) for their customers to stick with them, and 2) to improve their productivity. But this only happens through an organization of committed, loyal employees.

CLIMATE CHANGE

It has been argued that happy employees lead to happy customers, which leads to greater revenue and market share. This virtuous chain of effects appeals to our sense of justice and fair play, the idea that good things result from doing good, so in our hearts most of us want this to be true.

Without question, there is some truth to this chain of effects. But we also know that if it were that simple, then the primary strategic objective of every company would be to make their employees ecstatic.

Of course, the reality is much more complex. Happy and loyal employees, in and of themselves, do not necessarily create improved business performance or profitability. Companies succeed by meeting customers' needs, and they meet customer needs, in part, through the creation of a set of business processes that provide value for customers, and the creation of a culture that supports these processes.

Creating these processes and this culture is infinitely easier with happy and loyal employees whose needs and rewards are aligned with fulfilling customer needs. Benjamin

Schneider, professor emeritus at the University of Maryland, calls this a "climate for service."

Professor Schneider defines a climate of service as "the shared employee perceptions of the policies, practices, and procedures and the behaviors that get rewarded, supported, and expected with regard to customer service and customer service quality." In other words, a service climate is the employees' perceptions of 1) how the business actually runs, and 2) the goals that the company appears to be pursuing based upon its policies, practices, and procedures. Those behaviors that are rewarded, supported, and expected tell employees what the company really believes is important. All too often, this is vastly different from what is printed in the mission statement and recruiting brochures.

Professors James Heskett, W. Earl Sasser, and Leonard Schlesinger of the Harvard Business School suggest four critical elements of employee performance in satisfying customer needs: capability, satisfaction, loyalty, and productivity.

1. **Capability:** Capable employees can deliver high-value service to customers. This implies that employees have the training, tools, procedures, and rules to deliver good service.
2. **Satisfaction:** Satisfied employees are more likely to treat customers better than their dissatisfied counterparts.

3. **Loyalty:** Loyal employees are more willing to suppress short-term demands for the long-term benefit of the organization. As such, they may, themselves, place a priority on good customer service. Loyal employees also stay with their organizations longer, reducing the cost of turnover and its negative effect on service quality.

4. **Productivity:** Productive employees have the potential to raise the value of a firm's offerings to its customers. Greater productivity can lower costs of operations, which can mean lower prices for customers.

All of these factors are interconnected. Giving employees the capability-enhancing tools, training, and procedures clearly impacts their satisfaction and productivity. But it is employee loyalty that mediates the relationship of these factors on a company's climate for service.

Schneider and colleagues have shown conclusively that the employee's loyalty-related attitudes precede a firm's financial and market performance. And there is a much greater payoff in working on improving the human factor than people think. Researchers at the University of Pennsylvania found that spending 10 percent of a company's revenue on capital improvements increased productivity by 3.9 percent. Investing that same amount in developing the employee capital more than doubles that amount to a whopping 8.5 percent.

MAKING THE LINK

It is one thing to *believe* that employee loyalty results in positive financial outcomes; it is quite another to quantify those outcomes. But if we are going to be able to resist our natural inclinations to focus exclusively on the short term in difficult times, then we need to get very good at understanding what the real implications of employee loyalty to the long-term health of our business are.

The place to begin is by asking, "Where am I?" By that we mean, what kind of service climate does the company have? How loyal are our employees really? Doing this requires that we meaningfully solicit feedback from all employees (management included). And we have to be willing to ask tough questions. For example:

- How do our managers' relationship styles impact the organization's service climate and employee loyalty?
- Does the company provide the necessary tools and training for employees to perform their jobs well?
- Is a commitment to serve customers rewarded and encouraged by the organization?
- Does the company demonstrate that it deserves the loyalty of its employees?

There will of course be other dimensions that are of concern for our particular organization or industry. The key is to identify those few, vital dimensions that are most essential for our success! Once these dimensions are identified, they must be measured in a clear, objective, and rigorous manner.

Once we know where we are, next we must tie this information to the performance drivers of our business. Typically, these come down to four things: productivity, employee turnover, customer loyalty, and revenue.

Each of these measures is tracked in some form in virtually every organization. And the ability to link each of these measures statistically to employee loyalty is relatively straightforward. The key is to aggregate employee data into groups that link meaningfully to turnover, customer loyalty, and revenue. (For example, a retail chain might find store-level analysis to be the most relevant unit, because customer loyalty and revenue is tracked at this level, and stores typically have semi-independent management.)

The correlation between employee-loyalty-related attitudes and business outcomes is always meaningful from a practical, managerially relevant perspective, so it is worth the effort. In fact, a large-scale study conducted by researchers Harter, Schmidt, and Hayes presented compelling meta-analytic evidence that employee-loyalty-related attitudes were positively linked to each of these performance drivers. Furthermore, managers can learn a great deal by studying the performance of their most loyal business units, and how this is influenced by managers' own relationship styles.

Despite the ability to pull this information together to gain invaluable managerial insight, most companies do nothing (or next to nothing) in this regard. The number one problem in making the link isn't that this information doesn't exist. It is simply a lack of management will to pull the data contained in various departments together.

Why? The problem here is often a lack of desire to hear bad news. And without question, this kind of company internal examination always yields bad news. The reality is that employees are only as loyal to the company as they believe the company is loyal to them. This is true almost everywhere in the world! So in the end, building an organization of committed, loyal employees ultimately comes down to demonstrating to employees that the company deserves their loyalty.

Loyalty to Our Employer = Our Employer's Loyalty to Us

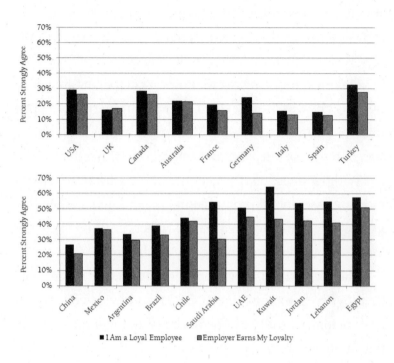

Source: Ipsos Loyalty

The Why of Customer Loyalty for Companies

Do what you do so well that they will want to see it again and bring their friends.

—Walt Disney (1901–1966), multiple Academy Award–winning film producer and co-founder of the Walt Disney Company

75

Why do businesses exist? The answer most businesspeople would give is "To make a profit." To quote Peter Drucker, widely considered the father of modern management, "This answer is not only false, it is irrelevant. . . . In fact, the concept is worse than irrelevant: it does harm."

Making a profit is how we know if companies are viable. But it is not why firms exist. Drucker summarized the purpose of business this way: "There is only one valid definition of business purpose: to create a customer."

Without question, Drucker is correct. Customers are the ultimate asset for all profit-making organizations. They provide all of a company's real value. Hence, creating loyal customers should be the aim of every business.

The good news is that managers have gotten the message that loyalty is good business. CEOs worldwide consistently cite customer loyalty as one of the (if not *the*) most important strategic objectives of their firms. Billions of dollars are spent each year by firms to improve customer loyalty. More than forty thousand books and hundreds of thousands (perhaps millions) of articles have been written espousing the profit-healing benefits of customer loyalty.

The bad news is that most firms' customer-loyalty initiatives are not living up to their promise. Where are all the happy, loyal customers? Customers in most Western countries don't feel very loyal to the companies where they do business. But they do feel that their loyalty equals or exceeds the loyalty shown to them by these businesses.

Customer Loyalty ≥ Company's Loyalty to Us

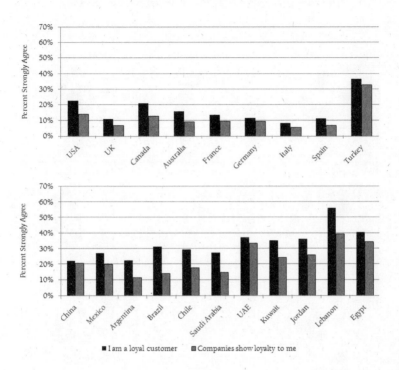

Source: Ipsos Loyalty

The reality is that most customer-loyalty initiatives have not proven to be good investment decisions. In fact, a look at the relationship between common loyalty metrics and the financial metrics managers actually use to run their businesses often appear completely unconnected.

Standard loyalty metrics don't link well to the financial metrics managers use to run their businesses.

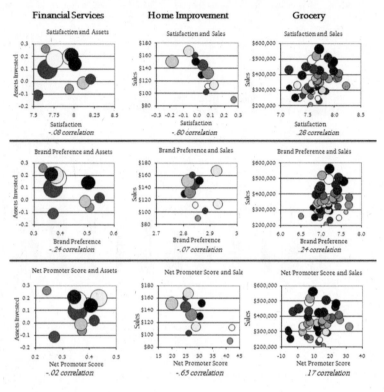

Size of bubble represents relative segment/district sizes.

Source: Ipsos Loyalty

Many readers are probably scratching their heads in confusion. If a customer-loyalty strategy isn't paying off for the vast majority of companies, then why should I care about loyalty?

Given the lack of success, it is tempting to discount the importance of loyalty. That is a mistake. Loyalty is requisite to the long-term success of any enterprise. A firm cannot survive without loyal customers. But managing loyalty for business success requires a holistic understanding of how loyalty and profitability align.

MORE THAN A FEELING

Too often, managers define loyalty solely as a feeling of attachment. But loyalty is about more than simply feeling a bond. Loyalty requires action. In this case, loyal customers continue to buy, allocate a higher percentage of their spending in the category, and willingly recommend the firm to others.

This in part explains why common loyalty metrics perform so poorly in linking to business outcomes. Most report on only one aspect of loyalty—how customers feel.

Why do they do this? First, getting a measure of how customers feel is relatively straightforward. All it takes is a good survey process to get an objective gauge of customers' attitudes. Second, there should be a relationship between how customers feel and what they actually do. Logically, if customers prefer doing business with a company, then there should be an increased probability that they will remain customers, purchase more, and recommend the firm to others.

The problem is that although both of these things are true, the strength of the relationship between how customers feel and how they behave tends to be relatively weak. This problem isn't solved by asking customers what they expect to do in the future (e.g., how likely are you to stay, buy more, or recommend the firm?). Measures of customer intentions are still based upon customers' feelings, and as such are inherently unreliable. And unreliable data often leads us astray.

Success requires that we know what customers actually do. The problem is that most companies do not have good information on their customers. Most do not collect data on their customers' purchasing behaviors. Of those few that do collect this information, fewer still use the information for much more than offering coupons or for reordering merchandise. And almost no firms link their customer survey information with their customer behavior data.

Typically, managers use their current lack of customer behavior information to justify relying on purely attitudinal data to gauge loyalty. Without question, collecting customers' purchasing data presents challenges in many industries. But managing customer loyalty without a means of assessing customer behavior is akin to playing a musical instrument without being able to hear the sound—there is no way to be certain that our actions produce the desired outcome.

Fortunately, there are ways to get insight into customers' buying behaviors. In the best of cases, each customer transaction is collected and stored electronically, and tied to a specific customer. But in the absence of such data, other options are still available.

Often, it is possible to build a panel with a representative sample of customers and monitor their purchasing behavior. These customers can also be surveyed to gauge their attitudinal loyalty to the firm, allowing for a complete picture of their loyalty.

When it is not viable to build such a panel, customers can be surveyed to ascertain both their attitudinal loyalty and their buying behavior (as opposed to their future intentions). Wherever possible, stated customer behavior data should be validated and calibrated with available internal data.

The data will rarely provide everything we would hope. But a means of gauging customers' behavioral loyalty is essential to making loyalty a viable business strategy. In the absence of perfect data, it is best to remember this management credo—"Don't let best get in the way of better!"

LOYALTY ≠ PROFITS?

Knowing how customers feel and how they actually behave allows us to gauge the firm's level of loyal customers more accurately. It is simply the percentage of customers who both feel loyal and act loyal (e.g., give the majority of their share of wallet to the firm when making purchases in the category).

Unfortunately, this definition of loyalty stills suffers from a serious drawback. It makes no distinction between customers who spend a lot in the category and those who spend very little. Customers who purchase very little are much more likely to give a higher share of their wallet to a single firm. Imagine someone who only purchases one item. That person has given 100 percent of their wallet to the firm. Clearly, a customer who dedicated a much lower share of his wallet to the firm but purchased more items would be much more important to the financial health of the firm.

The most pernicious problem with this view of loyalty, however, is that a very large percentage of loyal customers are not profitable for most firms. In fact, often more than 50 percent of loyal customers are not profitable.

Most readers now probably think we've lost our minds. We argue that loyalty is the right strategy for companies, and by *right* we mean the most profitable strategy. And now we argue that the majority of loyal customers frequently are not profitable. How can this be?

Well, the first thing we need to understand is that customer loyalty can be driven by different things. Often, customers are loyal because the services they receive far outstrip the cost to deliver these services. Customers are not doing anything wrong in accepting these services—firms typically provide these without determining their economic viability when bundled with other services used by loyal customers. Loyal customers also know enough about the company's offerings to recognize a good deal—and sometimes the promotions managers make are very bad economically for the firm.

For example, one financial services firm with whom we worked had very happy, loyal customers. The only problem was that more than two-thirds of these customers were extraordinarily unprofitable. Their loyalty was driven largely by their belief that their relationship with the firm resulted in exceptional deals on their products. Without question, the deals were exceptional—they were often mispriced. Every time the firm mispriced its offer, these customers bought in large quantities. So not only were these customers unprofitable, they were also some of the firm's largest.

This story illustrates two basic truths. First, there is no substitute for understanding the profitability of your customers. Customer economics for most firms strongly impact the linkage between loyalty and profits. Typically, most customers do not produce an acceptable rate of return (i.e., they are not profitable). Researchers at the Harvard Business School consistently find that the top 20–30 percent of customers generate all of the profits for a company. The bottom 20 percent loses money. And the middle 50–60 percent of customers just break even.

The trouble with this distribution is that loyal customers exist in each of these segments. And because the vast majority of customers are not profitable, often the majority of loyal customers are not profitable either.

Second, companies need to understand what it is that makes their customers loyal. For some customers, their loyalty is driven by things that aren't good for the business at all, such as in the case with the financial services company. Therefore, managers need to identify those customers who are truly served by the company. In other words, their needs are met at a price that allows the company to continue to fulfill those needs.

PROFITABLE LOYALTY

The ultimate aim of any customer-loyalty strategy is improved financial performance. Although loyalty and profitability are not diametrically opposed, they do not have to be aligned either.

To keep the two aligned, customer value must always be factored into any customer-loyalty analysis. This, however, demands that we change the way we view customer loyalty. Force-fitting customer value into typical 2×2 strategic planning grids masks important considerations.

Two-dimensional views of loyalty mask important differences.

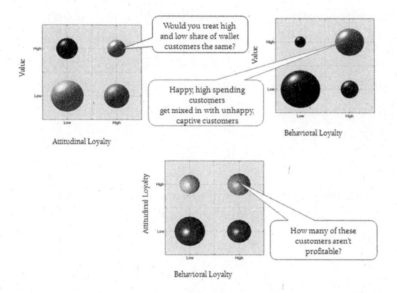

Source: Ipsos Loyalty

For example, if we examine the relationship between behavioral loyalty and customer value, our ideal customers using this framework are a mixture of customers who feel loyal to the firm with those who feel that they are held hostage. Similarly, if we look at attitudinal loyalty and customer value, our grouping of ideal customers combines customers who consolidate a large share of their spending with the firm with those customers who give a smaller share of their wallet. Clearly, we need to have a more granular view.

Managing for profitable loyalty requires a multidimensional view of customer loyalty. Attitudinal loyalty, behavioral loyalty, and customer value are three distinct, integral dimensions of customer-loyalty management. Using this framework, it becomes clear which customers are Profitable Loyals (i.e., they are high on attitudinal loyalty, behavioral loyalty, and value). It also becomes clear which of the firm's profitable customers are at risk, which customers have the potential to become Profitable Loyals, and which customers do not.

A three-dimensional view reveals which customers are truly loyal and profitable.

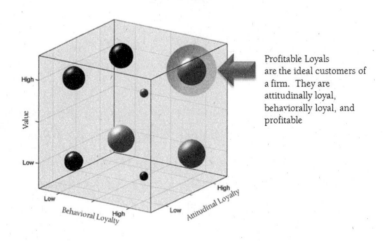

Profitable Loyals are the ideal customers of a firm. They are attitudinally loyal, behaviorally loyal, and profitable

Source: Ipsos Loyalty

Because customer value is built into the loyalty framework, focusing on measures to improve the number of Profitable Loyals keeps the goals of improving loyalty and financial performance synchronized. As such, tracking the percentage of Profitable Loyals a firm has among its customer base tends to be much more strongly correlated to firm financial performance than other commonly used loyalty metrics.

Tracking the Number of Profitable Loyal Customers' Links to the Financial Metrics Managers Use to Run Their Businesses

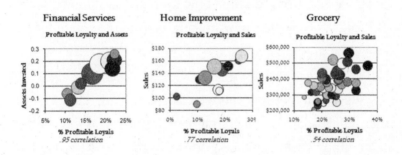

Size of bubble represents relative segment/district sizes.

Source: Ipsos Loyalty

The concept of Profitable Loyals has the added benefit of reducing the seemingly complex, multidimensional construct of customer loyalty into a simple, easy-to-understand gauge of how well the company is doing in aligning the needs of its customers with the needs of its shareholders. It does not take a rocket scientist to understand that profitable, loyal customers are the goal of every business, and that the greater the number of Profitable Loyals, the healthier the firm.

DRIVING CHANGE

Although knowing the percentage of Profitable Loyals provides insight into the well-being of a company, it is not the one and only number you need to know to improve customer loyalty. Instead, the Profitable Loyals percentage is akin to a thermometer reading—i.e., knowing our temperature can indicate that we have a fever, but it is not a diagnosis and treatment.

So, while we need to know our current performance level, we also need to know how to improve our percentage of Profitable Loyals. Unfortunately, getting the right answer is seldom as simple as asking customers, "What can we do better?"

We are not simply interested in knowing what makes the majority of customers happier (although we certainly want happy customers). Instead, we need to know what distinguishes Profitable Loyals from customers who have the potential to be Profitable Loyals. This requires that we recognize two things about our customers.

First, not every customer can or wants to be a Profitable Loyal. Some customers will always be price driven. Other customers purchase so little or so infrequently that even if they only purchased products in our category from us, they would never cover their costs. And some customers will always demand so much in service that, regardless of how much they spend with us, they will cost more than they contribute. Therefore, we must identify those customers that can legitimately become Profitable Loyals.

Failure to distinguish between customers results in an uninterpretable analytic mixture for accurately deriving what drives profitable loyalty. Worse still, given that Profitable Loyals are often in the minority, even among loyal customers, an undifferentiated examination of customer loyalty will be weighted to break-even and unprofitable customers.

Second, we need to recognize that Profitable Loyals are a mixture of many different types of customers, each with distinct needs and motivations. Consequently, we need to group customers into relevant customer segments based upon similar characteristics and needs. Otherwise, we end up regressing to the average when deriving what is important for improving profitable loyalty. Because no one is average, nobody gets what they really want.

Customer segmentation adds another essential element to the loyalty mix. Although it might seem that adding a fourth dimension would add complexity, the truth is quite the opposite. The customer landscape usually becomes much clearer in multiple dimensions. It is much easier to assess which customers are the best prospects for becoming Profitable Loyals, which customers contribute significantly to the firm's profits but are at risk because they feel no loyalty to the firm, and which customers are unlikely ever to become Profitable Loyals.

Segmentation makes it easier to identify customers more likely to become Profitable Loyals.

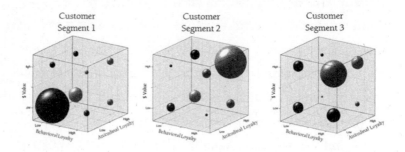

Source: Ipsos Loyalty

Once we know who has the greatest potential to become a Profitable Loyal, we need to determine what it will actually take to make that happen. For most firms, improving profitable loyalty is largely driven by increasing the share of spending that low-share customers provide to the firm. The key here is to understand why these low-share customers are allocating the bulk of their spending elsewhere.

Inevitably, common themes will emerge among potential Profitable Loyals regarding what is restraining their spending. Armed with this information, it becomes relatively simple to prioritize efforts to improve loyalty based upon whether the issue is easy or difficult to address versus the expected impact.

GETTING TO THE DESTINATION

Creating and nurturing customer loyalty is at the core of business strategy. Doing this, however, requires satisfying customer needs and wants at a sustainable profit. Too often, customer-loyalty experts have ignored the latter in the belief that loyalty and profitability are synonymous. Unfortunately, the reality of the marketplace has irrefutably shown that this is not true.

So what is a manager to do? How do you manage something that is multidimensional, and meaningfully simplify it in a way that everyone can easily grasp and rally around?

Remember the goal—improved profitability through customer loyalty. Make certain that what you measure and manage aligns with that goal. The path to sustained profitability through loyalty begins with creating more Profitable Loyals among your customers.

Profitable Loyals are the foundation upon which all thriving companies are built. They are most aligned with the company's mission and offers. And they are the customers who sustain the financial health of the firm.

The Why of Employee Loyalty for Me

We are all products of our environment. We are all affected by the people with whom we come in daily contact. We are all a part of all we have met. How vital it is, then, that our working associates—with whom we spend so many of our precious days—be of the finest character.

—Frederick W. Nichol (1892–1955), former general manager of IBM

Several years ago, this question was entered on Yahoo! Answers: "I was wondering, why should employees be so faithful and loyal to companies who don't care about them?" The best answer, chosen by voters, began this way: "Employees are not loyal, nor should we be. If we can get $5 more an hour for the same job by switching, most of us would. And why shouldn't we?"

This exchange demonstrates the quid pro quo of today's company–employee loyalty. As workers, all too often we find ourselves considered disposable. Not surprisingly, our loyalty as employees to the firms where we work has responded in kind. While this might seem totally fair, it doesn't make us feel any better. Our loyalty as employees directly impacts our happiness. We are much more likely to be happy if we feel strongly loyal to our work.

Our loyalty as employees impacts our happiness.

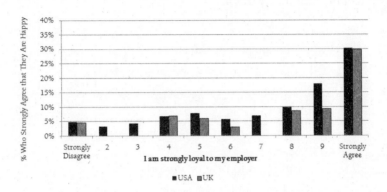

Source: Ipsos Loyalty

A lack of employee loyalty means we spend the bulk of our waking hours trading our time and labor for one thing only—money. Sure, we need to pay the mortgage, keep food on the table, etc. But if the only reward for our work is monetary, then the exchange is likely to leave us unfulfilled. The reality is that our research shows that things like "feeling you accomplish something worthwhile at work" and "feeling a deep sense of belonging to the company where I work" are far more important to most employees in driving their happiness than is pay.

If our work is making us unhappy—and as a result, we cannot bring ourselves to feel loyal—then we need to do some serious introspection. Is it really that the company "doesn't care," or is it something else? Clearly, not all work environments are conducive to our happiness. But frequently the problem is not the company per se, but our place in it.

Here are two of the most common problems with our ability to feel enriched at work:

1. The roles expected of the job
   a. What is it about my work that drains me?
   b. What aspects of my work do I love doing?
   c. How can I do more of what I love and less of what I hate?
2. Our connection to others at work
   a. What is the quality of my relationships with my peers?
   b. What is the quality of my relationships with my direct supervisors?
   c. What is the quality of my relationships with those who report to me?

Both of these issues are important. But it is our *loyalty* to others at work (our peers, supervisors, and direct reports) that most strongly impacts our overall happiness through our work.

So the belief by some that employee loyalty is dead, or an anachronism best left to a bygone era, is absolutely, without a doubt, wrong. Loyalty is critical both to a company's long-term success, and to our own happiness. As famed management expert Tom Peters observes:

> I think loyalty is much more important than it ever was in the past. Today loyalty is the only thing that matters.

But it isn't blind loyalty to the company. It's loyalty to your colleagues, loyalty to your team, loyalty to your project, loyalty to your customers, and loyalty to yourself. I see it as a much deeper sense of loyalty than mindless loyalty to the Company Z logo.

We spend far too much of our lives working not to derive some pleasure from it. But doing so requires that we build strong connections with others. And strong connections are built on loyalty.

The Why of Customer Loyalty for Me

I understand why people go on the Internet to find the cheapest flight or why they go out of their way to get the best deal on a car. I understand the desire to save money. But over a period of time, I believe that the loss of real human contact affects people. I do worry that my children are growing up in a world where every decision is being made on the basis of efficiency. We are removing a lot of the human element.

—James Carville, American political consultant

We live in what scientists and commentators refer to as the "consumer economy" with a corresponding "consumer culture." Recently, social scientists have come to recognize that this culture is impacting more than just our economy.

Birgitta Svensson, professor of ethnology at Stockholm University, observes that what is now viewed as the "new ideal human being has a great deal in common with the perfect consumer, who constantly needs new things, despite the fact that there is nothing wrong with the old ones." And renowned sociologist Richard Sennett declares that this type of consumerism is turning us into "tourists" as opposed to residents in our interactions with others:

> The consumer seeks the stimulation of difference from goods which are increasingly homogenized. He or she resembles a tourist who travels from one clone city to the next, visiting the same shops, buying the same products in each. But he or she has traveled: for the consumer, stimulation lies in the very process of moving on . . . changing one's desire becomes, like traveling, a kind of spectacle; it doesn't matter that the things one buys remain the same so long as one can sense oneself shifting . . . [I]n the new kind of consumption . . . surrender of an object is not experienced as a loss. Rather, abandonment fits into the process of finding new stimulations.

While Professors Sennett and Svensson view this as a bad thing, others view it as the ideal of modern life.

Professor James Twitchell of the University of Florida believes that shopping has become the ultimate "meaning-making act" of life today, carrying with it an almost spiritual significance: "Whereas the Heavenly Host organized the world of our ancestors, the Marketplace of Objects does it for us; they both promise redemption: one through faith, the other through purchase."

And in *The Happiness Myth*, noted author Jennifer Michael Hecht argues, "Money can buy some happiness. . . . Consumerism has become the culture's central opportunity for public performance; for being someone."

Twitchell and Hecht are correct that we do this to make ourselves feel better—to make us happy. Numerous scientific studies conclusively prove it. And the reality is that buying things really does make us happy. But for how long? This kind of happiness tends to last a few short minutes, frequently just a few seconds. Seriously! Researchers have shown that our happiness is likely to fade even before we make it to the car to take our things home.

This approach to happiness comes with real dangers. We teach ourselves that happiness rests in a self-consuming passion. For example, research finds that about 7 percent of the people of Hong Kong are shopaholics, who go on spending sprees to be happy.

The obvious truth to such a passion is that the new quickly wears off and the old shines through. This is the face of materialism. As psychology professor Tim Kasser observes, "people with strong materialistic values have significantly lower empathy, more competitiveness, more Machiavellian tendencies, and less generosity, and engage in fewer pro-social behaviors . . . Materialism undermines a healthy society."

Let's be clear. There is nothing wrong with buying things. In fact, we could not survive in the modern world without doing so.

But *things* tend to not make us happy for very long. Shared experiences do. Most of us fail to make this connection with regard to our buying behavior. We do not see the benefit in building relationships with companies. In fact, it can be argued that the idea is absurd, given that firms are profit-making entities, not human beings.

But the truth is somewhat different. We interact with employees of the company, not an abstract enterprise. These individuals become the face of the company to us. We can think of the process of our interaction as a kind of *customer journey*. Over time, we can develop real relationships that are tested with each encounter.

Sample Customer Journey

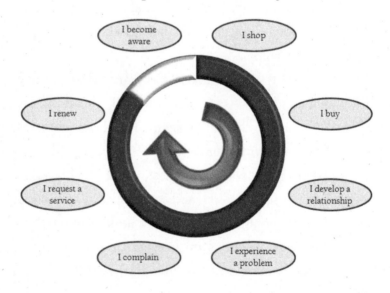

Source: Ipsos Loyalty

By developing relationships, our identification with these companies changes. It becomes *my* bank, *my* restaurant, *my* dry cleaner. At some level, we become more comfortable and familiar in our environment. As a result, this connection benefits us in ways that go beyond the simple economic exchange of goods and services for money. Our loyalty as customers directly impacts our happiness. We are much more likely to be happy if we feel strongly loyal to the places where we do business.

Our loyalty as customers impacts our happiness.

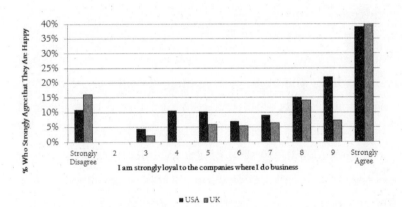

Source: Ipsos Loyalty

My Child's Life

Traditional thinking pits work and the rest of our lives against each other. But taking smart steps to integrate

work, home, community and self will make you a more
productive leader and a more fulfilled person.
—Professor Stewart Friedman, Wharton School of the
University of Pennsylvania

What does the future look like? This is a question that we all ask ourselves, but we seldom act as though we can affect the outcome. So instead we lament the decline in loyalty, and treat the loss of real human interaction as inevitable.

The opportunities that have been afforded to us by our economic prosperity are tremendous. It would be difficult to argue that the human condition is not better as a consequence. But clearly it is not without cost.

Many of us can recall times when service was a part of our regular interactions at work and where we shopped. Our parents and grandparents often thought of their careers as lifelong bonds with their companies. And they shopped, banked, and ate in places where people knew their names, and showed warmth and concern. While this demonstration of loyalty may not seem exciting or important, Josiah Royce, esteemed Harvard professor of philosophy, argues that it is this very kind of loyalty that is essential for our world to be in harmony:

[This] kind [of loyalty] isn't so exciting, yet takes a lot of character to see it through. In a way it is more important. The hundreds of faithful duties we must do every day are eloquent examples of—shall we call it pedestrian?—loyalty. It makes the world go around.

While this kind of loyalty has not completely disappeared from our lives, its decline to us as employees and as consumers from the peaceful days of the not-so-distant past has been considerable. That is because our economic environment removes the things we do not really value. We simply refuse to pay for them, so they become too costly for companies to include.

Clearly, we do not recognize the real value of loyalty, as we allow it to decline all around us. While we may mourn the loss of a company that provided us with outstanding service, the odds are that we siphoned off important pieces of our business with them in search of a better deal.

What is the benefit of a trend that leads us to further alienation simply as the result of how we work or buy? Can we comfortably imagine a future where our children reflect back on their lives and say, "This is exactly how it was when I was a child" to describe a world devoid of loyalty? Of course, none of us wants this. But this is the inevitable conclusion if we do nothing.

We are not suggesting abandoning the system (i.e., capitalism for socialism or some other "ism"). What we are saying is that we cannot allow the human aspects of our lives to be undervalued—this will only lead to its ultimate elimination and our future alienation. Loyalty is the manifestation of our common humanity.

We all have a responsibility to include loyalty in the economic equations of our lives—as managers, employees, and consumers. As managers, we must recognize (in more than an abstract way) that we have a responsibility to create organizations that foster loyalty for our employees and our customers. To do this, we must demonstrate that this is the right decision economically and ethically. And we must meaningfully demonstrate this to our shareholders in the down times of a business cycle so that they can willingly support the right decision to maximize the long-term value of the firm.

As employees, we must recognize that our work is much more than a means of putting food on the table. Our loyalty to our co-workers and to the cause for which we work influences us in ways that extend far beyond the workplace. It helps shape our identity, influences our psychological health, and connects us to others.

Finally, all of us are consumers. We need to recognize that our behavior as consumers has the potential to erode loyalty in all aspects of our lives. In fact, that is exactly what we have allowed to happen.

The future is not written. We have a say in how it unfolds. And if loyalty is to play a prominent role in that future, then we must recognize the profound impact of our economy and our jobs on the way loyalty manifests itself in society . . . and more importantly, how it manifests itself in us.

We are not helpless cogs in the machine. The economy exists to serve us—to provide us with the things we value. Therefore, we ultimately control how the economy behaves. If we truly value loyalty—meaning we will pay for those things that enhance our loyalty—then the market will respond.

It is up to us to decide what we really value . . . because you get what you pay for!

Chapter 5

Toxic Loyalty

Damn your principles!
Stick to your party.

—Benjamin Disraeli (1804–1881),
former British prime minister

L oyalty is the force the binds us together. It allows our civilization to have order and provides much of the meaning in our lives. But like virtually all things in life, loyalty is a double-edged sword. It can be used as a force for good or evil.

Without question, it is possible to be a loyal Nazi, Klansman, mobster, or gang member. It is also quite possible to be a loyal but abused spouse, a loyal but ill-treated employee, or a loyal but persecuted citizen. It would be difficult to argue, however, that loyalty in these circumstances presents the key to happiness and harmony in one's life.

Philosopher Immanuel Kant argues that all human desires and inclinations can be misused, and even the greatest of virtues can turn to vice at the extremes. Take love, perhaps our most heralded virtue. Though idealized as a source of strength and inspiration in poem, prose, and song throughout recorded history, it is unfortunately not difficult to find stories of love gone tragic. It's no accident that some cliffs are known as "Lovers' Leaps." Famed singer/songwriter Sting succinctly captured love's dual healing and destructive properties with, "Love can mend your life, but love can break your heart."

Unfortunately, 60 percent of us report having relationships to which we feel loyal that damage our emotional and psychological well-being. The majority of these relationships are with family and friends. Not surprisingly, having such relationships significantly lowers our happiness.

Percent of Population with Some Degree of Toxic Family or Friend Relationships

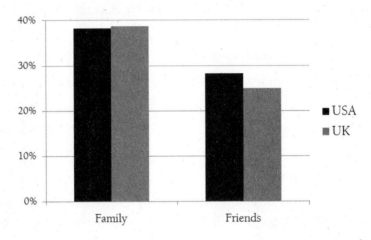

Source: Ipsos Loyalty

Some toxic loyalties have the potential to damage even more than our happiness. They have the potential to tear at the fabric of our communities . . . even society at large. History is filled with evils committed in the name of loyalty to something or someone. Sadly, we still witness tragedies caused by misguided loyalties.

Like love, loyalty can bond our communities and enrich our lives. But when misdirected, loyalty can corrode our communities and char our souls. But just as we do not give up on love when we learn of its failures, renouncing the need for loyalty is equally unacceptable. It is vital, however, to recognize when loyalty brings strength and when it is toxic.

Loyalty to the Dark Side

The success of *Pirates of the Caribbean* is a testament to our romanticized history of pirates. And if all pirates were as appealing as Johnny Depp's portrayal of pirate captain Jack Sparrow, our love affair with swashbuckling and rollicking pirate tales would be well placed. But the reality is that pirates were a motley crew of vicious criminals. Despite their violent nature, pirates were known to demonstrate strong loyalty to their ships. In fact, the Pirate's Code, often idealized in adventure novels and movies, is a genuine code that was adopted by a seventeenth-century band of pirates in the Caribbean known as the Brethren of the Coast.

Pirates followed a long tradition of almost-legendary loyalties associated with criminal groups. And the tradition would continue with criminal organizations such as the Mafia, Yakuza, and Triad, all well known for their tenets of loyalty. It is no accident that the expression "thick as thieves" denotes the closest of bonds.

Clearly, loyalty to a group or to individuals who support criminal activity directly harms society. But in demonstrating that loyalty, in being supportive of such activity, the individuals themselves are also harmed. Far beyond the simple threat of being arrested or incarcerated, loyalty among thieves can eat at one's humanity as it demands viewing others as prey, as sustenance. The resultant contagious behavior of such a mindset is that of Frankenstein's monster: anti-social, untrustworthy, and often dangerous.

Fortunately, most of us recognize and reject the inherent dangers of criminal loyalty. And while the dream of being a rebel who rejects the conventions of society will always hold some appeal in our imagination (à la James Dean and Marlon Brando), we know in our hearts that the fantasy is far better than the reality.

But there are times when the dark side calls to us, and we are forced to elect an unpopular, or even anti-social, path, in order to prevent abandoning the "correct road." And sometimes, knowing the difference between the two, between good and evil, can be nearly impossible. The dark side can be provocative, even masquerading as something as venerable as patriotism; here, the call for loyalty is the sirens' call:

> I swear by God this sacred oath that I shall render unconditional obedience to Adolf Hitler, the Führer of the German Reich and people, supreme commander of the armed forces, and that I shall at all times be ready, as a brave soldier, to give my life for this oath.

In the twenty-first century, these chilling words evoke the ghost of an eerie, sinister monster whose megalomania and cruelty threatened much of Western civilization. The memory of Hitler's insanity is despised the world over, and even those who did not experience Hitler's brutality first-hand remain strict in their abhorrence. Recently, an Austrian man found himself sentenced to two months in jail for using a version of the "Hitler Oath" as a greeting for his cell phone voice mail.

But in 1934, this oath evoked quite different feelings among the officers of the German army who pledged it; it evoked a sense of patriotism and duty. And a major reason that so few German officers turned against Hitler—despite his harsh treatment of German soldiers, his unsound military strategy and tactics, and all of the crimes committed under his orders—was this vow of loyalty.

It is difficult to fathom a more just defeat than that of Hitler's Nazi regime. As a friend and German military officer once told one of the authors, "I'm glad we lost the war—I'm not kidding." Nonetheless, in the 1930s and 1940s, loyalty to Adolf Hitler not only made Nazi victory desirable for millions but a cause worth dying and killing to achieve.

Fortunately for most of the world, loyalty to Darth Vader–like evil is so obviously wrong to us that such lunacy is more likely to be considered a trait of ignorance than an alluring temptation. Loyalty to hate groups is so unacceptable that it borders on the absurd. And given its absurdity, such loyalty lends itself as source material to comedians for some of their most humorous routines.

For example, the very first episode of Dave Chappelle's popular comedy show, "Chappelle's Show," contained a spoof of the PBS series *Frontline*. It featured a biography of Clayton Bigsby, a blind white supremacist, who was the author and leading voice of his movement. Ironically, his blindness prevents him from ever having known that he is black. The episode ends with the interviewer sadly noting that, upon learning that he is African American, Mr. Bigsby filed for divorce from his wife of nineteen years because, euphemistically, she loved a black man.

The irony of Bigsby's loyalties put a spotlight on the ridiculousness of racism and served to demonstrate humorously the self-destructiveness of loyalty to principles based upon a hatred of others. As Chappelle's comedy sketch reminds us, you often find that you become what you hate.

Unfortunately, calls for loyalty that prey upon our worst fears and suspicions still plague us. One prominent example is the so-called *Stop Snitchin'* movement that has become widespread in many inner-city communities throughout the United States.

Stop Snitchin' is a popular hip-hop slogan that means "Do not cooperate with the police for any reason." As CBS News's *60 Minutes* reports, "the message appears in hip-hop videos, on T-shirts, Web sites, album covers, and street murals. Well-known rappers talk about it endlessly on DVDs. It is a simple message heard in African-American communities across the country: don't talk to the police."

What was once perverted loyalty to a code of silence— one that was limited to criminals who were caught by the police—*Stop Snitchin'* is now being marketed as the cultural norm in poor communities, with devastating consequences. Cold-blooded murders go unsolved because witnesses refuse to betray this loyalty. It has become a major roadblock to stemming lawlessness in many U.S. cities.

"I don't know what frustrates me more . . . these knuck-leheads killing each other, or the residents who won't coop-erate with my officers," sighs one frustrated police officer. Observes another officer, "No one wants to be accused of snitching . . . these people have become so desensitized to the violence, it's almost become a way of life."

Clearly, the *Stop Snitchin'* movement embodies a philoso-phy of misguided loyalties. A pro-criminal, anti-social cul-tural norm is best left to the world of science fiction novels, but it permeates our inner cities nonetheless. And it serves as a real-time reminder of the ever-present threats posed by loyalty to the dark side.

While we can all agree that ethnic prejudice, racial preju-dice, or pure lawlessness are patently evil, we also know that such evil is rarely so obvious. Loyalty to the dark side is typi-cally more convoluted. In fact, loyalty to the dark side is often disguised as a proof of love or belonging, a means to achieve a greater good, or even demonstrated devotion to God. But a wolf in sheep's clothing is still a wolf, and virtually all the faults of loyalty are a result of loyalty to the dark side.

Blind Faith Loyalty (Spiritual)

Most of us believe in things that cannot be proven by science. In fact, we, the authors, are happy to go on record as saying that many of the things we believe in most strongly and hold to most fervently make no sense scientifically. To quote Emily Dickinson, "'Faith' is a fine invention."

But faith can have a dark side. Our inherent need to be part of something larger than ourselves has the potential to override our reason. Karl Marx, author of *The Communist Manifesto*, famously remarked that "religion is the opiate of the masses." Without supporting Marx's generalization or his aims in making this statement, we can extend Marx's analogy further; when faith becomes fanaticism, it mimics an addiction. Nothing else matters, and we make poor choices to support it.

Killing in the name of God has blighted mankind throughout human history. And, unfortunately, we still live in a world where a few believe that their faith provides them with moral superiority and entitles them to act as the righteous hand of God. They fancy themselves as the world's judge, jury, and executioner.

But the irony of God "needing" someone to carry out His work for Him is clearly lost on the fanatical. For the nerds among us (the authors include themselves), it is reminiscent of a famous response by Captain Kirk (from *Star Trek*) to an ethereal being pretending to be God who demanded use of the starship USS *Enterprise*: "Why does God need a starship?" Or as a comedian joked, "If your God needs you to kill for Him, how weak is your God?"

Adherents of virtually every religion believe that *their* way is *the* way. This is perfectly fine. And while it is nice to imagine that all religious faiths will one day see beauty and value in their counterparts, this is not the world in which we live. This also is perfectly fine. But when loyalty to our faith demands subjugating outsiders (those who do not share our beliefs) either to our will or to our wrath, then we have chosen the dark side. And this is not fine. Period!

Blind loyalty has not only led some to kill but some to die in His name. Mass suicides led by charismatic religious leaders make obvious just how far "true believers" are willing to go in the name of their faith. They are willing to make the ultimate sacrifice.

In 1997, we were shaken to learn that thirty-eight members of the Heaven's Gate religious group had committed suicide. Their leader, Marshall Applewhite, convinced his followers that by doing so their souls could take a ride on a spaceship that was hiding behind the Hale-Bopp comet. This ship, alleged Applewhite, carried Jesus on board.

Perhaps the most notorious example in recent history of following a spiritual leader's call for mass suicide involved members of the Peoples Temple group at the Jonestown settlement in Guyana. The leader of the group, Jim Jones, commanded that members commit suicide after U.S. Congressman Leo Ryan and members of Ryan's entourage were killed on orders from Jones. More than 900 people died, 276 of them children. Most died by drinking cyanide-laced Flavor-Aid (commonly misidentified as Kool-Aid). As a result of this tragedy, a new phrase entered the American lexicon: "drinking the Kool-Aid." It is used to describe fervently and blindly following a belief to the point that defies good judgment.

Today, we all recognize the senselessness of the tragedy that occurred at Jonestown. Fortunately, Stephan Jones, the son of Jim Jones, did not commit suicide with the group because he was playing basketball with members of the Peoples Temple in a competition against the Guyanese national team. Stephan is now married with three children, and clearly does not mourn the death of his father. But in an interview aired as part of the documentary, *Jonestown: Paradise Lost*, Stephan acknowledged a chilling insight. Had he been in Jonestown on this horrible day, he fears that despite his disillusionment with his father and his strong desire to live, he very likely would have followed the group to his own death. Not letting down his community held such importance that death may have at that moment appeared preferable.

All religious faiths have the potential for blind faith among at least a portion of their followers. And in light of tragedies such as Jonestown or Heaven's Gate, one thinks of them quietly as cults, rather than bona fide religious circles, because of their fanaticism. But think for a moment . . . if irrefutable evidence was obtained that the core tenets of one or all of the world's religious faiths were shown to be overtly false, would this spell the complete end of these religions? It could certainly cause many to abandon their faith. But would everyone abandon the faith?

We already know the answer by looking at doomsday-based cults. When they witness an objectively apparent falsification of their beliefs (i.e., the world did not end when it was supposed to end), does this fact cause the belief to be abandoned? The answer is a resounding *no*. Prophecies do not fail for the committed. In fact, believers rationalize the event, aided by "1) marginal goal modification, 2) the welcoming of imitator-prophets, and 3) increasing proselytizing activity in order to ascertain social support."* In other words, the failure of their prophecy actually results in increasingly vocal support for the faith by its most loyal followers.

Fortunately, most use their religious faith as a means of leading better lives. By *better* we mean lives of compassion, forgiveness, and love toward our fellow man. The overwhelming majority of us consider the idea of causing harm

---

* Neil Weiser, "The Effects of Prophetic Disconfirmation of the Committed," in *Expecting Armageddon: Essential Readings in Failed Prophecy*, ed. Jon R. Stone (New York: Routledge, 2000), 106.

to another in the name of God repulsive. The same holds true for suicide in God's name. And while many religions espouse an ultimate end-of-the-world prophecy, most followers leave this in God's hands and focus on improving themselves and their communities.

Blind Faith Loyalty (Psychological)

Extreme examples of blind faith loyalty are not limited to religion. M. Lamar Keene coined the term *true believer syndrome* to describe people's continuing belief in paranormal activity after it was proven that the events were staged. There are numerous examples of this occurrence.

Psychologists Victor Benassi and Barry Singer conducted an experiment in which Craig Reynolds was brought in to fake a psychic performance. Participants were told in advance that Reynolds was a magician and that the performance was staged. Even so, more than 50 percent of participants indicated that they believed they had witnessed genuine psychic activity despite being told that they were witnessing a magic trick.

In 1988, a man named José Alvarez toured Australia claiming to channel a 2000-year-old spirit from Venezuela named "Carlos." (*Channeling* is the term for a procedure where the spirit of someone deceased enters the body of an individual so that the spirit can speak through this individual.) Carlos's Australian tour ended with a large-scale event before an enthralled audience at the Sydney Opera House.

Afterward, the hoax was exposed. But even after exposing the charade, many people still believed in Carlos.

While many would like to comfort themselves by deriding the gullibility of these examples of blind faith, the truth is that on some level we all suffer from this exact ailment. Just because we would not commit acts of violence in the name of God or reject clear evidence of fraudulent paranormal activity does not mean that we are immune from blind faith loyalties. We differ only in degree.

In fact, we experience blind faith loyalties all of the time. Anyone who has ever been assigned to an obviously doomed project at work, one that is championed by management, has experienced blind faith in action. Despite overwhelming evidence to the contrary, the company's management cannot envision the project failing, and the same thing happens with our loyalties. We have all known individuals who remain loyal to friends, spouses, or ideals even after being presented with overwhelming evidence of untrustworthiness and betrayal by the object of that devotion.

In fact, we WANT to believe. It is hardwired into our brains. Researchers in psychology have found that the human brain holds on to the most rewarding view of events, and our minds selectively invest in "facts" that conform to our views, even in the face of conflicting information or outright contradiction of our beliefs. Clinging to our firmly held notions is a basic human tendency, and it impacts all aspects of our lives; our loyalties are no exception.

While blind faith loyalties do not necessarily lead us to loyalties to the dark side, when we suspend reason for loyalty, we abdicate the personal responsibility that living freely demands of us all. Therefore, when making our choices, it is imperative that we distinguish between what we believe based on fact and what we want to believe based on faith. As Galileo offered, "I do not feel obliged to believe that the same God who has endowed us with senses, reason, and intellect has intended us to forgo their use and by some other means to give us knowledge which we can attain by them."

Partisan Loyalty

If I had to choose between betraying my country and betraying my friend I hope I should have the guts to betray my country.

—E. M. Forster (1879–1970) "Two Cheers for Democracy" (a.k.a. "What I Believe")

These words are shocking, even treasonous. Like most extreme positions, there are obvious cases when supporting friend over country is the morally acceptable choice, and other times when such a decision is clearly immoral. During World War II, the Nazi resistance was comprised of a few brave souls who risked their lives to save Jews and ethnic minorities from Nazi concentration camps, and they certainly made the morally acceptable decision by ignoring patriotic propaganda.

In the United States, G. Gordon Liddy, a principal culprit in the Watergate scandal who considers himself the most steadfast of patriots, refused to inform on his co-conspirators. However, even Liddy, believing that the crimes he committed on behalf of ex-President Nixon were acts of patriotism, has his limits of allegiance. When asked under what circumstances he would have cooperated with authorities, he replied, "well, only if I stumbled upon the fact that [Nixon] was betraying the country to the K.G.B. or something like that."

But few would regard Terry Nichols's support of his friend, Timothy McVeigh, in preparing to destroy the Murrah Federal Building in Oklahoma City as morally acceptable. Clearly, it is impossible to justify helping a friend in causing the death of 168 innocents, some of whom were children who were in the daycare center on the first floor of the building.

Thankfully, the lose–lose situation of choosing friend over country is a rhetorical hypothetical. The fact is that in free societies—although we all have at some point complained about our governments' policies, practices, and procedures—the governments we have are the ones we voluntarily created through our votes. While attaining a "government of the people, by the people, for the people" has not always been achieved, "governments are instituted among men, deriving their just powers from the consent of the governed." In other words, in free societies, the government is "we the people," flaws and all.

But why is it that we actively tolerate leaderships that are decidedly flawed, sometimes bordering on idiocy? The answer is that we further demonstrate our loyalty to the system and challenge the leadership itself to uphold their end of the social contract. In fact, democratic systems allow room for public criticism, with no one considered untouchable. Former U.S. President Theodore Roosevelt declared, "to announce that there must be no criticism of the President, or that we are to stand by the President, right or wrong, is not only unpatriotic and servile, but is morally treasonable to the . . . public." And it is this obligation, to monitor and critique your government, that identifies public need and rallies the public's will for change. Far from perfect, according to Sir Winston Churchill, "democracy is the worst form of government, except all the others that have been tried."

The success of government is based upon the faithful performance of those who are entrusted with the honor and responsibility of representing the people. These leaders must be loyal to the supreme laws of the land, as well as to the people who elected them, by acting on behalf of the best interests of their constituency. More often than not, however, when the words *loyalty* and *government* are mentioned together in a political context, *loyalty* becomes a euphemism for *party loyalty*. In other words, the representative tends to follow the initiatives and policies of the political party to which that individual belongs.

This is not to suggest that there is anything inherently wrong with loyalty to a political party. Political parties have existed for hundreds of years, and they serve a valuable purpose. They provide a common platform to address issues of importance to a significant portion of the population.

Obviously, there is nothing wrong with having an ideology. Furthermore, there is nothing wrong with disagreeing with another ideology, particularly when the objective is to "secure the blessings of liberty to ourselves and our posterity." But disagreement does not mean disagreeable. Elected officials have a duty to work for the betterment of society. As a result, even majority opinions must not be used to oppress those in the minority. Therefore, compromise and honest discourse are the only viable alternatives. Such is the nature of a political life; such is what is necessary to be a part of the "Loyal Opposition."

Furthermore, parties help provide guidance to voters as to the ideology of the person running for office. As Michael Kinsley notes:

> Many or most of the decisions that an elected official must make on your behalf aren't even known when you must decide whether to vote for him or her. An ideology functions like a pledge or a promise, and it allows you, the voter, to judge the politicians seeking your vote in two different ways: their politics and their character. Do you share his or her political principles? And does he or she stick to them as new issues arise? Without some kind

of ideology, the politician is asking voters to buy a pig in a poke.

Problems arise, however, when partisan loyalty supersedes loyalty to the people they swore to represent or the supreme laws they have sworn to uphold. One newspaper journalist describes the state of his government as a "group of failed, selfish, preening and disconnected Has-Beens and Never-Will-Bes [that] have decided their own feuds are more important than trying to remove a destructive Government." Interestingly, this observation could be used to describe the recent political environment in many countries.

Partisan politics is nothing new. And while most of us despise partisan practices, cries of partisanship being the worst in a country's history are typically melodramatic. Often, a country's worst historical partisanship occurs before an attempted rebellion, coup d'état, or even outright civil war. Fortunately, rebellion and civil war are not things most of us in Western society are seriously worried about.

At its worst, partisan politics risks tearing a country apart based upon political ideology. It closes our mind to the failings of our own party, and views the actions of those outside the party as misguided, if not sinister. As George Orwell observes, "The two-party loyalist not only does not disapprove of atrocities committed by his own side, but he has a remarkable capacity for not even hearing about them."

Partisan hacks at their worst will impersonate loyal, passionate public servants, reminiscent of the totalitarian regimes of which free societies are supposed to be polar opposites. To quote Orwell again, "totalitarian systems . . . instill beliefs that are firmly held and widely accepted although they are completely without foundation and often plainly at variance with obvious facts about the world around us." That statement works equally well if we substitute *partisan hacks* for *totalitarian regimes*.

But extreme partisanship does not end with elected officials. In fact, practicing political partisanship would be a futile exercise were it not for its pervasiveness in our news organizations, our primary source for real information to make informed decisions.

Comedian Jon Stewart, host of the parody news program *The Daily Show*, strongly criticized the media during an appearance on CNN's *Crossfire*:

> You are partisan hacks. You're doing theater. What you do is partisan hackery. You have a responsibility to the public discourse and you fail miserably. This is such a great opportunity you have here to actually get politicians off their marketing and strategy.

Stewart, judged to be honest and approachable in the eyes of today's twenty- and thirty-something crowd, has slowly become a legitimate political force in today's media circus and has the backing of millions of fed-up U.S. residents. His actions on *Crossfire* were largely received with a supportive cheer, indicating that people have grown tired of being symbolically disenfranchised by the politicians who they elect, as well as by those who peddle the rhetoric for these politicians.

It seems, at least to his viewers, that Stewart is one of the few people trying to honor the loyalties of the American public by keeping the political debate in this country as honest as he can. Unlike politicians, at least he's trying. And perhaps, Stewart would likely say, we should expect less of our comedians and more of those running our government.

Partisan loyalties blur the lines of normalcy. We learn that partisan politics will do anything to succeed for the sake of itself, even creating fictional accounts of reality in order to dodge responsibility or paint the opposition as vile. Such behavior, it is plain to see, has clearly crossed over to the dark side. As Kinsley notes, it's clear what the people want: "They want an end to partisan bickering. They want pragmatic solutions, not ideological posturing. They want leaders who reject politics as usual and put the country's interests ahead of the party's. They want a government that will do the right thing, regardless of whether it is 'liberal' or 'conservative.' They don't like labels. And, oh yes, they are tired of spin." AMEN!

Discrimination Loyalty

"Birds of a feather flock together." This common English phrase, dating back to the sixteenth century, encapsulates an idea as old as mankind itself: We prefer the company of those like ourselves. Our preference to be surrounded with those like ourselves is not only a function of our cultural heritage; it is a function of evolutionary factors at work. Researchers have found that there is a "sizeable genetic component to our tendency to seek out people like ourselves."

This cultural and evolutionary bias, which helped ensure our survival as a species, comes with some unfortunate consequences. Historically, humans have shown a strong disposition to magnify differences amongst themselves, to discriminate or even subjugate one another if deemed to be not enough alike. Many of mankind's greatest civilizations were dependent on conquering and enslaving laborers who were just sufficiently different from themselves. Thankfully, the evil of de jure slavery is considered a violation of international law (though debate remains regarding de facto cases). And while we still have a long way to go before we stamp out prejudice and discrimination, we have come far in our recognition that we have much more that unites us than divides us.

Despite our progress in this regard, we are still far more likely to surround ourselves socially with people of similar interests and backgrounds. In this regard, we *do* discriminate. And as we seek our mates, we are allowed to be as discriminating in our selection as we want. Politically correct or not, we are hardly outraged by someone saying something to the effect of: "I am attracted to 1) fair/dark skin, 2) blond/brunette/red hair color, 3) brown/blue/green eyes." The problem develops when our natural propensity toward being comfortable with people similar to ourselves interferes with an overriding need for equal treatment for everyone.

This same premise applies to the role of loyalty in our lives. We are more likely to show loyalty to individuals who share our interests and backgrounds (i.e., people like us). And as such, the tendency to surround ourselves with those who have demonstrated loyalty to us, in certain instances, can potentially evolve into loyalties of the dark side.

Rarely in real life are dark-side loyalties on greater or more frequent display than in the case of cronyism in the history of politics. Throughout the history of government (of any type), there have been innumerable instances where a leader has elected to populate important governmental roles with those who have previously demonstrated strong personal or professional loyalty, regardless of their qualifications to handle the responsibilities of the roles allocated to them. This is one part of cronyism.

A second part of cronyism is when being nominated as part of a leader's supporting cast prevents legitimate competition from being considered for that position. Cronyism is a corrupting dark side of loyalty. Paul Waldman, former associate director of the Annenberg Public Policy Center at the University of Pennsylvania, observes, "[the] unswerving fealty to whatever [a government leader] happens to want to do demonstrates one danger of loyalty, the fact that if its object is less than virtuous, the result is the inevitable corruption of the loyal subject."

Even historically acclaimed political leaders have succumbed to cronyism. U.S. President Franklin Delano Roosevelt, the only American president to serve more than two terms, was accused of appointing people of doubtful qualifications to government posts based upon the loyalties of these individuals.

Instances of political cronyism leading to dire situations can and do happen, such as in the case of the appointment of Michael Brown (former FEMA Director during Hurricane Katrina, who was hired by his long-time friend, then-FEMA Director Joe Allbaugh, as FEMA General Counsel before ultimately being appointed FEMA Director). Appointing unqualified individuals to important positions clearly does not serve the public interest, and it betrays the loyalties of the constituency to do so.

Cronyism can also imply a perverted view of loyalty that is based on blind obedience to a leader. But as Paul O'Neill, President George W. Bush's first treasury secretary, noted after his resignation, "That's a false kind of loyalty, loyalty to a person and whatever they say or do, that's the opposite of real loyalty, which is loyalty based on inquiry, and telling someone what you really think and feel—your best estimation of the truth instead of what they want to hear." And when obedience supersedes the objective of your position, then that is a true sin.

The sins of political cronyism can extend beyond the scope of appointed positions to include the corrupt (or nearly corrupt) assignment of government contracts. When cronyism extends to awarding government business to loyal favorites, the consequences can be disastrous. As one journal reports, "Besides giving a privileged few obscenely huge gains at public expense, cronyism discourages investment by the great majority of firms which don't know people in high places. That translates into slower economic growth, lower government revenues and fewer jobs. [Furthermore] scandals over shady deals can destabilize governments and unseat national leaders."

The problems of cronyism are also relevant in our everyday work environments. We have all been witness, at some point, to favoritism at work. And while employee loyalty is clearly a good thing, a superior's favoritism toward a subordinate—based on their relationship and not on their qualifications—is not. Favoritism in exchange for personal loyalty can be a corrosive and far-reaching poison. Nonetheless, the practice rages on. Renowned film producer Samuel Goldwyn once remarked, "I'll take 50 percent efficiency to get 100 percent loyalty." Unfortunately, 50 percent efficiency just might be the price for some organizations.

The organizational performance of a company is at risk once cronyism infects the organization, as it is diametrically opposed to meritocracy. Once merit is no longer correlated to rewards, employees find that there is no incentive to improve. And the company suffers because when competence is not required for success, there is no incentive to improve. As a result, organizations rife with cronyism are not efficient enough to withstand the demands of a competitive environment.

Instances of cronyism must give us pause as they remind us of the awesome power that loyalty wields. Many leaders have intentionally forgone what they knew to be in the best interest of their organization (or their country) in order to surround themselves with birds of their feather.

So should we populate governments with public servants and companies with employees that feel no loyalty whatsoever to the people who hired them? The idea is preposterous. But loyalty cannot override justice in social institutions without harming the organization or, at times, even the whole of society.

Emotionally Unsustainable Loyalty

Friends love misery, in fact. Sometimes, especially if we are too lucky or too successful or too pretty, our misery is the only thing that endears us to our friends.

—Erica Jong, American author

*Friends broaden our horizons. They serve as new
models with whom we can identify. They allow us to be
ourselves—and accept us that way. They enhance our self-
esteem because they think we're okay, because we matter
to them. And because they matter to us—for various
reasons, at various levels of intensity—they enrich the
quality of our emotional life.*

—Judith Viorst, American author

If we look at the people in our lives, which of the two pre-
ceding statements would best describe those with whom we
surround ourselves? Hopefully, all of us have experienced
the friendship of individuals who elevate us and help us to
become the best person we can be, the person we were born
to become. Chances are, though, that we have also had relationships that were soul-sucking experiences.

A Turkish proverb warns that "a good friend can make
you a 'vizier' (second only to the king), or a disgrace." Life
teaches us to be careful when it comes to deciding who
to befriend. And life also teaches us that the people with
whom we share our time can greatly influence how we see
ourselves, present and future. Strangely, we spend very little
energy seriously reflecting on this point. How often do we
stop and think . . .

- Who are we communicating with most?
- Who is having the greatest influence on our
  thinking?

132

- Are these the people we want to be like?
- Is anyone a negative influence?
- Is anyone a positive influence?

The fact is that most of us have the opportunity to choose with whom we spend our time. And negative is negative, positive is positive. We aren't suggesting that you abandon certain people entirely. We are suggesting, however, survival first.

Motivational speaker Steve Pavlina sums up the issue this way: "What about loyalty? Shouldn't you always be loyal to your friends? Once you have a close friend, even if their influence on you is somewhat destructive, shouldn't you stick by them? . . . [The answer:] Loyalty to a friend sometimes means having to let go. It means being loyal to their highest and best self as well . . . True loyalty sometimes requires that you break destructive connections, get yourself back on solid ground, and then decide what you can really do to help your friend (which sometimes requires letting them hit bottom)."

This was the strategy employed by Frank Sinatra that saved his friendship with, and probably the life of, fellow Rat Packer Sammy Davis Jr. When Sinatra could no longer bear Davis's drug use, he acted out of true loyalty and love by confronting Sammy. "'Look,' Sinatra said, 'God put you here for a lot of reasons that you and I don't even know about. He gave you a talent, and you're abusing it. And I'm watching my friend go down the tubes. I loved you when you were nothing. I'll love you when you go back to being nothing. But you're cheating yourself. You're cheating your friends, and you're cheating your public. So long as you're going to do that, then I don't want to be around you.' . . . Sammy heard Frank's message. He promised to quit doing drugs, and he kept his word."*

If your loyalty to a relationship influences you negatively, then the relationship is toxic. While it may be repairable, it is not sustainable in its current form without damaging you.

Calculative Loyalty

Sometimes, loyalties are decided by simple economic calculus; given the cost of disloyalty to a particular individual or group, we simply choose our loyalties based upon tangible value. By calculative loyalty, we refer to loyalty that is spawned out of the necessity to battle threats (real or perceived), as well as loyalty that is maintained because the cost of switching loyalties would involve personal sacrifice.

Calculative loyalties are usually marriages of convenience, often driven by the desire of two groups to strengthen their position against a common enemy. History (ancient and modern) is filled with large-scale examples of such loyalty. In the fifth century, Attila the Hun built a fierce fighting force largely driven by the sharing of plunder.

---

* Gary Fishgall, *Gonna Do Great Things: The Life of Sammy Davis, Jr.* (New York: A Lisa Drew Book/Scribner, 2003), 312.

Sixteen centuries later, Afghan warlords notoriously switch allegiances based on the strength of the opposition and economic incentives; the United States used this to their advantage in overthrowing the Taliban.

The American Revolutionary War was won with such calculative loyalty. The American colonies, seeking independence, secured the loyalty and aid of another British foe, the French. In fact, were it not for French support, the American forces would most certainly have been defeated and the Founding Fathers of the United States (George Washington, Benjamin Franklin, Thomas Jefferson, etc.) would have been found guilty of treason and faced execution. Therefore, the debt to France should have been particularly high, especially because funding this war seriously depleted the French treasury.

But as the American Revolutionary War demonstrates, the problem with calculative loyalties based on challenging a common enemy is the tenuous nature of such relationships. When the mission of American revolutionaries had been accomplished, the tangible benefits of mutual loyalty disappeared. Given that calculative loyalty is based on tangible value, parties will tend to look out for what is in their best interest. The French discovered this the hard way.

The colonies negotiated directly with England, completely leaving France out of the discussions. Benjamin Franklin shrewdly convinced the French that this was an error based on inexperience in such matters, and that

Britain would not come between France and the new United States. Franklin further convinced France to provide his new country with additional funding. In terms of maximizing the benefits to the United States, Franklin's calculative loyalties rank supreme.

While it is clear that calculative loyalty greatly benefited the new nation of the United States (and economically harmed the French monarchy), calculative loyalties often have unintended, negative consequences. For example, the United States' arming of the Mujahedeen to fight the Soviet Union in Afghanistan was a testament to the potential perils of calculative loyalty. When the Soviet Union ultimately withdrew, so too did the need for Afghan–American loyalties. The result was the Taliban and the rise of Osama bin Laden.

Of course, most of the calculative loyalties we experience in our lives are not of historic consequence. But they frequently are of great personal significance. The difficulty is in achieving our aims without selling out.

Loyalties of the "you scratch my back, and I'll scratch yours" variety are not inherently bad. In fact, international diplomacy is heavily based on the notion of reciprocity. But we need to acknowledge the risks of developing loyalties of this kind. If we do not anticipate how the value in this loyalty equation will change and how the loyalty itself will subsequently morph, we run the risk of underestimating the true cost of fostering such a relationship. Such a risk often results in the later realization of just how toxic relationships can be.

Systemic Loyalty

To avoid the pitfalls of toxic loyalty, we must differentiate between the healthy limits of loyalty and the level at which loyalty turns rancid and threatens us through our own human frailties. In most cases, we can clearly see the difference between right and wrong, good and evil. This is in great part due to our socialization process, during which we are exposed to the blessings of our society's system of checks and balances, a system that we come to rely upon as the foundation of our inner moral compass. The system itself helps to prevent us from wavering in situations of turmoil. Where unnerving actions are present, we usually rely upon the written laws of society to guide our disposition. Certainly, there are instances where "lesser" laws are pliable, but even that pliability has limits. Few of us abhor traveling 2 mph over the speed limit, but we are (or at least should be) wary of traveling 40 mph over it. We rely on the system to keep us safe and to guide us toward a prosperous and protected life.

Today, we recoil at the thought of Hitler's disgusting impact on the face of history. We assuage our collective conscience by convincing ourselves that, if magically teleported into the body of a German military officer in the early 1940s, we would act out against the Reich. We would sabotage it, crusade against it, warn people about the true nature of Hitler's intent. Whatever it took to stand against it, we would endeavor to do it. We cannot imagine that we would be jaded by vile loyalty to the dark side. We would choose instead to be virtuous. But if research into human behavior holds any insight, however, this might be wishful thinking.

Social psychologist Stanley Milgram conducted now-famous experiments into the willingness of people to commit unspeakable acts upon others when told to do so from someone in a leadership role. At Yale in 1961–62, Milgram had individuals administer electric shocks to another person under the pretext of examining the effect on our ability to learn. This pretense, however, was false. In fact, Milgram was studying our willingness to inflict harm on others when told to do so by someone in a position of authority. Fortunately, no one was actually being shocked; instead, an actor dramatically acted out the role.

In the experiment, participants were told to deliver a shock to an unseen respondent if the respondent answered a question incorrectly. The voltage was increased for each subsequent response that was incorrect, and this continued until the voltage reached an identified lethal level. When Milgram surveyed others, who were not participating in the experiment, only 4 percent indicated that they would administer a potentially lethal jolt. However, the results from the actual experiment were quite different. Approximately

65 percent of participants administered what seemed to be a lethal shock, despite their counterpart's desperate pleas for mercy.

Would the results change if the experiments were conducted today? Based upon the evidence of other researchers who have attempted to replicate Milgram's experiments, the answer appears to be a resounding *no*. Thomas Blass examined Milgram's experiments and their replications over a twenty-five-year span, from 1961 to 1985, and he found no relationship whatsoever between the year the research was conducted and the level of "obedience" exhibited. And women and men were equally likely to inflict harm.

Sadly, most of Milgram's participants experienced genuine anxiety at being instructed to inflict potentially lethal harm, spurring ethical debates in social and physical sciences alike. And while the ethics of the experiment might have been questionable, the results certainly were not. Despite the anxiety participants felt, they pressed the button anyway. Their blind loyalty to authority of the system outweighed their personal, moral objections.

Of course, we recognize that in some societies (and unfortunately in some relationships), the risks associated with not conforming, despite moral convictions otherwise, can be extremely harsh, even perilous. Our hearts break when we see individuals in such situations punished for their refusal to conform to the demands of an oppressor. We are not so arrogant as to argue that those who face peril have no right to choose survival. Therefore, we must distinguish between obedience under duress and loyalty.

Virtuous Loyalty

Loyalty has the power to be ghastly and the power to be supreme. Therefore, we need to distinguish between toxic loyalty and what we call "virtuous" loyalty. Virtuous loyalty is "balanced" loyalty that co-exists with what Columbia law professor George P. Fletcher called the need for "impartial justice" and "rational discourse." In his essay on the need for loyalty, Fletcher ends by imploring:

> The challenge for our time is uniting the particularist leaning of loyalties with the demands, in some contexts, of impartial justice and the commitment, in all contexts, to rational discourse. As much as I make this plea for loyalty, I make a stronger plea for the qualities of mutual respect and reasoned discourse that make this or any argument worthwhile. There is no point to an argument that would be accepted or rejected on the basis of personal loyalties.

The contrasts between virtuous and toxic loyalty are as stark as responsibly taking a medication prescribed to heal our bodies, as opposed to an addict's dependence upon a narcotic as a means of temporary psychological escape from the realities of life at the expense of his physical and mental health.

Mankind has committed some of its greatest evils either under the guise of loyalty or by misusing the notion of it. Various types of toxic loyalty permeate the inner fabric of our society and eat at the foundations of some of our most trusted institutions. Those who zealously insist on the loyalty of others, or offer loyalty to others with ill intent, actively contaminate the vital role that loyalty plays. Loyalty draws its power from our innate, human ambition to share a bond with our friends, our lovers, our families, our community, our country, and our God. But toxic loyalty pollutes society, so we must understand that loyalty should never be unconditional. And if we correctly lay our trust and loyalty toward those who deserve it, loyalty is a beautiful thing. But we must delineate between healthy loyalty and toxic loyalty.

Examples of toxic loyalty are rarely as straightforward as the fight against fascism. It is commonly difficult to identify, as in Milgram's experiments, where the line must be drawn between behaviors that stretch the spirit of the system to which we cling, and which behaviors betray the spirit. This leads to the most important rule of virtuous loyalty: NEVER, EVER IGNORE YOUR MORAL COMPASS.

We acknowledge that some do not hear the same moral voices. Sociologist Amitai Etzioni observes:

> People who live in closed societies, subject to extensive and prolonged religious or political indoctrination may not hear the same moral voices as speaking to them as self-evident truths. However, once these societies open up

or people from isolated segments of our own societies are exposed to free dialogues they also hear the same limited moral claims. When you go to societies where dialogue is suppressed, and people have been indoctrinated whether via imposed religion or imposed cultural traditions they often do not hear the truth of which I speak. But when their societies open up, after a period of dialogue, they gradually gravitate toward the same truth.

Most of us in the West do not live in closed societies. Therefore, when confronted with a choice between adhering to the letter of an ideal, or to the spirit of an ideal, you should endeavor to choose the latter. For example, the soldier who disobeys a direct order because he believes it to be patently illegal or immoral has remained loyal to the spirit of the system that he is sworn to defend, rather than to a to-the-letter application of the system's rules. This is not to say that the soldier is "right" one way or the other by exposing himself to arrest. That is a situational judgment, and there is not always a decipherable "right" or "wrong" in every case (especially in a military context). We are not saying that your compass will always be perfect, but at least you will make choices your conscience can live with.

Most of us reading this book enjoy the blessings of liberty, but with those blessings come real responsibilities. To whom much is given, much is expected. We have all faced pressure to do something with which we did not feel comfortable in order to fit into a social role, to make or keep friends, or to please someone in a position of leadership. It is in such circumstances that our own moral compass must take precedence, and we must let that compass indicate where the acceptable boundaries are in a given situation.

This in no way implies moral superiority to those who choose not to conform in such circumstances. For example, adherence to a particular religious code of conduct is one's right and must be shown consideration, but this consideration in no way implies that those who believe differently are morally inferior. Like the dissenting soldier, an individual who listens to his own moral compass must accept sole responsibility for his actions.

Given that we are ultimately responsible for the decisions we make, it is imperative that we strive to make good decisions. But virtuous loyalty is a concept, not an equation. And following our compass can occasionally lead us astray—even if our intentions are virtuous—inadvertently leading to toxic loyalty. Most often, our loyalty is toxic when we are forced to choose between competing loyalties and we simply make the wrong choice.

For example, Robert E. Lee, leader of the Confederate armed forces during the American Civil War, actually supported the union of the United States. In 1861, Lee opposed the secession from the union of his home state of Virginia. Furthermore, though once himself a slave owner, Lee outwardly recognized the evil of slavery. In a letter to his wife, he wrote, "in this enlightened age, there are few I believe, but what will acknowledge, that slavery as an institution, is a moral & political evil in any Country."

Despite these sentiments, Lee rejected an offer by President Abraham Lincoln to command the U.S. military (i.e., Union) forces and chose instead to side with "his kith and kin" (friends and family) of his home state of Virginia when the state voted to secede. Moreover, he accepted Virginia's call to command all of their forces, ultimately becoming General-in-Chief of all forces of the Confederacy.

Although many might regard Lee as noble and heroic, it cannot be ignored that he fought for a cause in which the consequence of victory would have been the perpetuation of slavery in one of the last countries where the practice was still legal. After the defeat of the Confederacy, Lee rejected calls to continue the fight, writing, "so far from engaging in a war to perpetuate slavery, I am rejoiced that slavery is abolished."

While clearly the Civil War would have happened regardless of Lee's choice of sides, it was nonetheless a tragic decision. We can sympathize with Lee's loyalty to his beloved Virginia, and we can also argue the issue of "state's rights" as legitimate grounds for secession. But the reality is that had the Confederacy succeeded, slavery would most definitely have continued for many more years. As one of the authors takes great pride in his Southern heritage, he says emphatically (as did his German friend), "I'm glad the South lost the war—I'm not kidding."

Lee's misplaced loyalty was reflected in his own recognition that slavery "is a moral & political evil," yet he still chose his "kith and kin." Lee's loyalty to Virginia can be understood. But loyalty to any cause that has as a primary and intended outcome the proliferation of obvious evil is loyalty to the dark side no matter how it is cloaked. Our respect for Lee comes not because of his leadership of the Confederacy, but because of his regret and his efforts to help heal the United States after the war.

Like Lee, we all exist in a world of overlapping loyalties: to friends, family, lovers, country, and God, to name a few. Fletcher observes that the more abstract the loyalty, the less likely we are to choose this loyalty when it comes into conflict with a more tangible loyalty. For example, loyalty to family tends to supersede loyalty to society at large.

Clearly, a parent will choose to save the life of his or her own child over the life of another, regardless of the contribution of that individual to society. Of course, the loyalty is understandable. But even with parental loyalty, we have obvious limits to what we consider acceptable for a parent. While we sympathize with the parents of children who commit violent offenses against others, we also understand when these parents choose to turn them over to authorities to face the consequences of their crimes. In fact, we expect them to do this, even as we empathize with their pain.

So why the double standard? Why can you protect your child in one case and not in the other? Political philosophers might argue that the difference rests in the differing needs for justice in the two cases. Social philosophers might argue it rests in familial responsibility to the community at large. Without question, there is truth to these positions.

But we argue that the simple difference is that one is a situation of self-preservation, and the other is the obvious evil that is enabled by allowing these crimes to go unpunished. And as we noted earlier . . .

> LOYALTY TO ANY GROUP OR CAUSE THAT HAS AS A PRIMARY AND INTENDED OUTCOME AN OBVIOUS EVIL IS LOYALTY TO THE DARK SIDE NO MATTER HOW IT IS CLOAKED.

Most of the time, we all know right from wrong. Of course there are gray areas, but it is not the gray areas of loyalty that tend to create the greatest harm to society. Harm is done when we behave in any way that adds evil to our world, and that is often done under the pretext of loyalty to something or someone. And to ward off grand evil, we must first address the strength that evil gains from the loyalty of its concubines. When these are eliminated, then philosophers can debate the gray areas.

Until that time, NEVER, EVER IGNORE YOUR MORAL COMPASS.

Chapter 6

Faith and Loyalty

Love is, in some form or other, an essential to the spirit of loyalty, and it operates as the potent power in religion . . . Any form of religion that does not demand that love to God be practically expressed by love to one's fellows is but a useless shell.

—William Armstrong Fairburn,
American author

Research consistently shows that religious faith is associated with greater happiness. In fact, our own research finds that individuals who invest a great deal of themselves to enhance their spiritual selves are significantly happier than those who do not.

Religion is a uniquely human experience. We are the only species on Earth that shows any evidence of spirituality or religion; and every society has at some point in time practiced some form of religion. The recorded history of humankind—its literature, art, and architecture—reveals the overwhelming influence of religion on man's existence.

Throughout most of history, religion served to explain our universe. The inexplicable often became the miraculous. Today, however, many (if not most) of our superstitions for natural phenomena have been explained by science.

Yet we are still very much a religious people. Despite impassioned and often well-written pleas for an end to religion (although we do not agree with those pleas), mankind overwhelmingly holds to a belief in the supernatural. Eighty-four percent of the world's population professes a religious faith.

Philosopher David Hume argued, "the first ideas of religion arose not from a contemplation of the works of nature, but from a concern with regard to the events of life, and from the incessant hopes and fears which actuate the human mind." It is these concerns that cannot be assuaged by science.

Perhaps most important, religion links believers to one another, as well as to the eternal. It is often said that the universal question of mankind is *Why?* But it is also true that each of us will at some point ask *Is that all?* And for many, religion provides an answer to this question. We all want our lives to have meaning, and to contribute to something greater than ourselves. By its very nature, religious faith is a manifestation of loyalty—some would argue the ultimate manifestation of loyalty.

Religion and Loyalty

Today, most of us associate the word *religion* with a belief in the spiritual. Interestingly, the origin of the word is *to tie*.

Without question, religion promotes group unity. Members of many religious groups frequently think of themselves as belonging to a "family" of believers. In fact, many faiths refer to fellow believers as "brothers" or "sisters"; religious leaders are sometimes denoted as "fathers." Even God is frequently called "Father" or "Mother."

Therefore, religion can to some degree be thought of as an outgrowth of communitarian practices. There is loyalty both to God's voice and to the community of believers. In fact, it is the congregation that provides the framework for interpreting God's will. In his essay on loyalty, Professor George Fletcher writes:

> The foundation of the religious life is the acceptance of a higher power in the universe, and that acceptance, in turn, entails humility as a condition of the religious life. Humility requires that one hear the voice of God not as a self-proclaimed prophet but as one member of a congregation that tests its visions over time. Further, and more significantly, a congregational conception of religion mediates against the excesses of individuals who think they hear the voice of God. . . . Only those practices survive that contribute to the flourishing of the community and its members.

And while most religions are unique to a tribe or tribes, an ethnic group, or a nation, believers of all faiths tend to regard themselves as being part of one community, even if geographically, racially, and ethnically dispersed. For example, Islam uses the Arabic term *Ummah* to refer to the community of Muslims throughout the world. Similarly, Christianity uses the Latin term *Corpus Christianum*, "the Christian body," to describe the community of all Christians.

Insiders and Outsiders

Religious faith typically fosters a concern for the well-being of fellow believers. As Nobel laureate Herbert Simon observes, "Beliefs about rewards and punishments after death, which are present in one form or another in most religions, provide an important example of the support of altruism . . . [religions] often promise rewards for behavior that is altruistic."

This sense of altruism, however, frequently has not extended to outsiders. Virtually all religions underscore the differences between believers and non-believers. On one hand, this is understandable. If all religions are equally valid, then what is the point of committing to the sacrifices demanded of any particular faith? But an emphasis on religious differences has led to some of mankind's greatest sins.

An overwhelming desire to root out heretics and to convert or eliminate heathens ultimately leads to an out-group brutality. The horrors associated with the Spanish Inquisition, the conquistadores, the Crusades, and the 9/11 tragedies are testaments to the violence that is possible in the name of the divine. Sadly, as author Jonathan Swift observed, all too often, "We have just enough religion to make us hate, but not enough to make us love one another."

From Christianity to Christendom

Governments have long recognized the power of religion to secure the loyalty of citizens. A common religion provided a shared set of beliefs and goals, an overarching sense of community, and often a perception of the morality of believers (and the wickedness of non-believers). A common religion also helped to secure solidarity with neighboring states.

To further cement the link between God and country, rulers were often declared descendents of gods; for example, Alexander the Great claimed to be the son of Zeus. And if not gods themselves, ancient kings frequently asserted that their right to rule was derived from God and superseded the will of all others, including the will of citizens. Hence, this became known as the "Divine Right of Kings." Therefore, by uniting state with faith, rulers were able to commingle their desires with God's will in the minds and hearts of citizens. Consequently, religion became a critical element in the building of empires throughout most of recorded history.

While much of the spread of religions can be directly attributed to military conquests, the adoption of Christianity in Russia provides a more humorous insight into the seriousness with which rulers regarded state religion. In the late tenth century, Prince Vladimir of Kiev sought to establish a national religion to strengthen the loyalty of his people. At the time, Vladimir was a devout pagan, who enjoyed the company of numerous wives and 800 concubines. As a pagan, he chose to establish Perun, the god of thunder and lightning, as the supreme deity. To demonstrate his devotion, it is said that he offered hundreds of human sacrifices to the gods.

Ultimately, Vladimir came to believe that a "world" religion would have more power in building loyalty and civilizing his people. According to legend, Vladimir examined Judaism, Islam, and Christianity (Roman Catholicism and Eastern Orthodoxy). Judaism was rejected because Vladimir interpreted the loss of Jerusalem as evidence that God had abandoned the Jewish faith. Islam was rejected because of its prohibition against alcohol. Upon learning of the prohibition, Vladimir reportedly said, "Drinking is the joy of the Rus'."

As a result, Vladimir chose Christianity. He selected Eastern Orthodoxy because his emissaries found the Byzantine church (the Hagia Sophia in what is today Istanbul, Turkey) to be literally heavenly, stating, "They did not know whether they were in heaven or earth. They only knew that God dwells there among men. They could never forget that beauty."

Of course, whether or not there is truth to the legend, Vladimir clearly gained politically by this decision. It provided for an alliance with the Byzantine Empire that was sealed with a marital tie.

Separation of Church and State

Because of the long-standing connection between religion and government, most Western countries have historically had (or still have) one formally recognized state religion. Not only were these faiths officially sanctioned, but governments also provided extensive direct and indirect financial aid in support of their official state religions.

The United States is a notable exception. The Founding Fathers of the United States were secularists who believed in the separation of church and state. In fact, the Constitution makes no mention of God. As an article in the *New York Times* notes, "The men who wrote the Constitution labored for months. There's little chance that they simply forgot to mention a higher power."

The framers of the U.S. Constitution were not anti-religion. They were against a state-favored religion. Religion is the only area of the U.S. Constitution that the Founders singled out for protection from government interference. The Founders also strongly opposed allowing differences in religious beliefs to be a pretext for hostility toward other countries. This is clear in the words of the Treaty of Tripoli, drafted in 1796 under President George Washington, and signed in 1797 under President John Adams:

> As the Government of the United States of America is not, in any sense, founded on the Christian religion; as it has in itself no character of enmity against the laws, religion, or tranquillity, of Mussulmen [Muslims]; and, as the said States never entered into any war, or act of hostility against any Mahometan [Muslim] nation, it is declared by the parties, that no pretext arising from religious opinions, shall ever produce an interruption of the harmony existing between the two countries.

The treaty, endorsed by President Adams and Secretary of State Timothy Pickering, was ratified by the Senate. The vote was unanimous, making it only the third unanimous vote in Senate history at the time. Following its ratification, three newspapers reprinted the treaty in full: two in Philadelphia, and one in New York City. There was no public complaint recorded in later editions of these papers.

Paradoxically, while the United States is founded in secularism, it is one of the most religious countries in the West. England, on the other hand, with an established church headed by the monarchy, is one of the least religious countries. It is argued that the religious fervor of the United States is actually fostered by its secular constitution; because there are no constraints on religion, religions are free to prosper.

This logic would appear to be supported by Jawaharlal Nehru, the first prime minister of India. Nehru, a founding father of India's constitution, championed secularism and religious harmony:

> We talk about a secular [country] . . . Some people think that it means something opposed to religion. That obviously is not correct. What it means is that it is a State which honours all faiths equally and gives them equal opportunities . . . In a country . . . which has many faiths and religions, no real nationalism can be built up except on the basis of secularity.

Today, the overwhelming majority of citizens in Western democracies agree with the principles of separation of church and state. The observation of French historian and political thinker Alexis de Tocqueville regarding religion in America in the 1830s is particularly insightful: "They all attributed the peaceful influence exercised by religion over their country principally to the separation of church and state. I assert confidently that, during my stay in America, I did not meet a single man, priest or layman, who did not agree about that."

Religion, Democracy, and Pluralism

The question of the twenty-first century is whether the world's religions can be compatible with pluralistic democratic societies. Citizenship in any Western country carries with it both blessings and burdens. But for the faithful, it can present distinct challenges.

In rare-but-noisy cases, loyalty to one's religious beliefs may conflict with the demands of civil law. For example, the courts have been forced to rule on the use of illegal drugs in some religious ceremonies.

More typically, however, civil law often permits what a particular religion forbids. As a result, the faithful are forced to do their best to insulate themselves from temptation, and to encourage changes in the law. How this is done, however, can often result in conflict.

In *Public Matters: Politics, Policy, and Religion in the 21st Century*, William Galston, former deputy assistant for domestic policy to President Clinton, argues that there is a right and a wrong way for religion to contribute to public policy.

> The right way occurs when each faith tradition is regarded as a tributary nourishing the vast and heterogeneous expanse of . . . public culture, the body of understandings, norms, and aspirations from which we draw the premises of public dialogue. The wrong way occurs when a specific faith tradition asserts a comprehensive and unchallengeable dominion over all others, such that its premises and commitments enjoy dialogic primacy and are endowed with the force of law.

The growing diversity of religions within Western countries has brought with it a realization of the need by many faiths to accept religious pluralism. Harvard professor Bryan Hehir observes such a shift for Roman Catholicism:

> In the nineteenth century church–state controversies . . . religious pluralism was an exception to be tolerated when it could not be overcome . . . In the teaching of Vatican II religious pluralism was . . . the accepted setting in which the church pursued its ministry in freedom, dependent only on its own resources and the quality of its witness.

Not everyone is convinced, however, that the world's religions can peacefully co-exist. Many in the West openly question whether fervent devotion is compatible with pluralistic, democratic societies. In *The God Delusion*, Oxford University professor Richard Dawkins uses the extreme reaction of some to offenses that Western societies consider protected free speech as a manifestation of what he believes to be the inherent waste of religion in general. While we do not agree with this position, Dawkins makes a valid point: "if you don't take [their sensibilities] seriously and accord it proper respect you are physically threatened, on a scale that no other religion has aspired to since the Middle Ages." Of course, the vast majority of the faithful of all mainstream religions are repulsed by violence. Nonetheless, the threats of a dangerous minority are very real, and raise genuine concerns.

Without question, intolerance and brutality in the name of God are not compatible with democratic ideals. But we have every reason to believe that we can live together in peace. In fact, our forefathers have already proven that it can be done. From approximately 711 to 1492, a period referred to as *La Convivencia* (literally translated as *the Coexistence*), Muslims, Jews, and Catholics in Spain lived together in relative peace. The three faiths co-existed in a pluralistic society. They shared ideas and ideals with one another. They engaged in business with one another. And often, they even lived in the same neighborhoods. The resulting civilization was one of the most magnificent in history.

The lesson of La Convivencia is clear. We can live together! We can learn from one another! But to do that, we must communicate with one another, and respect the liberty of all—even those with whom we disagree. The words of Swiss Catholic theologian Hans Kung ring true:

> There will be no peace among the nations without peace among the religions. There will be no peace among the religions without dialogue between the religions. There will be no dialogue among the religions without common ethical standards, and there will be no survival of humanity without a global ethic.

Loyalty to the Eternal

It is often written that some version of the Golden Rule (i.e., treat others as you would like to be treated) appears in the faiths of all cultures. In fact, it has been argued that this is the fundamental truth we must learn through our faith. Hillel, one of the most important figures in Jewish history, observes, "That which is hateful to you, do not do to your fellow. That is the whole Torah; the rest is the explanation; go and learn."

Benjamin Franklin offers a similar observation:

I think vital religion has always suffered when orthodoxy is more regarded than virtue; and the Scriptures assure me that at the last day we shall not be examined for what we thought, but what we did; and our recommendation will not be that we said, Lord! Lord! but that we did good to our fellow creatures.

The aim of religion is to bond us to one another and to the eternal. In *The Philosophy of Loyalty*, esteemed Harvard professor of philosophy Josiah Royce argues that the pinnacle of loyalty is the same. Loyalty in its purest form is "the will to believe in something eternal and to express that belief in the practical life of a human being." As a result, "loyalty and religion may long keep apart. But the fact remains that loyalty, if sincere, involves at least a latent belief in the superhuman reality of the cause, and means at least an unconscious devotion to the one and eternal cause."

Chapter 7

Teaching Loyalty

The schoolroom is where loyalties first collide.

—George P. Fletcher, professor of
jurisprudence at Columbia University

What is it that makes a community? Geography? Race? Religion? Language? While each of these can play a role in uniting a people, they are not enough to ensure a cohesive society. A community requires a common identity.

Throughout history, it is the stories endlessly told—myth, history, poem, and song—that crystallized our view of the world and our place in it. Our ancestors were taught that they were part of something larger than themselves, that every person has value, and that we all belong. Our children must be taught this same lesson.

In his essay on loyalty, Professor George Fletcher observes,

> The teaching of literature, history, and civics provides the primary vehicle for casting this common identity. Pupils must not only speak the same language, they must come to rehearse the same books and poems, cherish the same national heroes, loathe the same villains, and develop common sentiments toward their shared institutions. That is what it means to live in a common culture.

What we are taught ultimately enables us to define who we are and our vision for society. It is these lessons that instill the values cherished by our communities. These ideals are not instinctive; they are taught. This is how we learn to be good citizens, to be contributing members of society. As such, schools are the greenhouse of a community.

Learning to Be Loyal

Benjamin Franklin believed that virtue was an art, but like most arts, virtue is not instinctive: "[One] must be taught the principles of the art, be shown all the methods of working, and how to acquire the habits of using properly all the instruments; and thus regularly and gradually he arrives, by practice, at some perfection in the art." The truth is that we all need constant training in the art of loyalty.

Loyalty by its very nature demands that we commit ourselves to a person, group, or cause. We suppress our short-term self-interests to maintain our bond. In its most noble form, we serve a cause greater than ourselves, designed to unite with another.

Therefore, in our training to be loyal, we need to learn the real meaning of service to something greater than oneself. In the words of Martin Luther King Jr., "The complete education gives one not only power of concentration, but worthy objectives upon which to concentrate."

Schools can help develop the art of loyalty in our children by incorporating service to the community into the curriculum—what is referred to as "service learning." Research on the impact of service learning shows that students who participate in high-quality programs become more civically engaged.

But simply including community service in the curriculum is not enough to instill the foundations of loyalty. This is starkly evident by the fact that sentencing someone to community service as punishment for a crime rarely instills greater loyalty to the community.

It is not enough simply to do. Instead, our children must come to understand, internalize, and cherish the virtue of doing.

Character Education

Loyalty demands maturity. While children can and do experience strong emotional ties, loyalty is the result of personal commitment. Therefore, young children cannot be expected to be loyal per se.

But young children can learn the preliminaries to loyalty such as responsibility, perseverance, and respect for others. These values are highly interrelated to loyalty and are part of the life lessons that we all expect our children to learn. As such, character education represents a critical responsibility of our schools.

The idea that schools should focus on instilling virtues in our children is not new. In fact, it dates back to the very beginning of education. For Plato, "education in virtue is the only education which deserves the name."

This belief that education is the conduit for a virtuous society has long been held by some of history's greatest philosophers. English philosopher John Locke observed, "of all the men we meet with, nine parts of ten are what they are, good or evil, useful or not, by their education."

The Founding Fathers of the United States held this same view. In fact, they rightly believed that for democracy to work, citizens must be educated and virtuous. The word *and* is critical. Education to improve the intellect of all citizens is essential but not enough. For modern democratic societies to succeed, it is essential that all children be educated, and that they be taught to cherish the values that we as a people hold dear. U.S. president and primary author of the U.S. Constitution James Madison warned, "To suppose that any form of government will secure liberty or happiness without virtue in the people is a chimerical idea."

Nonetheless, the idea that schools should seek to instill moral values is not without principled debate. Arguably, parents, not schools, should be the ultimate teachers of values to children. Without question, instilling virtues is first and foremost a parental responsibility. But U.S. Secretary of State Hillary Clinton is also correct—it takes a village to raise a child. She begins her book, *It Takes a Village*, by stating the inarguable truth:

> Children are not rugged individualists. They depend on adults they know and on thousands more who make decisions every day that affect their well-being. All of us, whether we acknowledge it or not, are responsible for deciding whether our children are raised in a nation that doesn't just espouse family values but values families and children.

While there are legitimate points for debate in her book, the core idea advocated by Clinton is neither liberal nor conservative. As conservative radio talk show host, columnist, and author Kerby Anderson acknowledged, "At its face, there is nothing controversial about the idea that it takes more than parents to raise a child. Grandparents, friends, pastors, teachers, boy scout leaders, and many others in the community all have a role in the lives of our children."

The role of the community in raising our children is as old as civilization itself. But the need has likely never been greater. The time pressures of modern society make the challenge facing parents in the teaching of virtue to their children daunting. This is compounded by the overwhelming amount of time that children are bombarded with conflicting, sometimes violent messages. Research indicates that children spend 1,500 hours per year watching television, but less than 40 hours per year in meaningful conversation with their parents. These numbers point to the difficulty that parents face, and the virtual impossibility of their being able to go it alone.

By their very nature, schools play a vital role in assisting parents in overseeing children's development. Children spend approximately 900 hours per year in school. And the reality is that schools cannot function without communicating values to their students. Students must come to value honesty, integrity, cooperation, self-improvement, and learning itself if education is to have any hope of success. As Edward Wynne, professor of education at the University of Illinois, argues, "Schools are and must be concerned about pupils' morality. Any institution with custody of children or adolescents for long periods of time, such as a school, inevitably affects the character of its charges." Therefore, it is not a question of teaching morals in school but of deciding which values to instill.

Despite much publicized debate, polls consistently show that we are concerned with the values that our children are being taught. And there is actually a strong consensus about the virtues we as a people hold dear. Research finds that greater than 90 percent of us believe that children should be taught honesty, acceptance of different races and ethnicities, love of county, moral courage, and caring for friends and family in the public schools.

Similarly, teachers overwhelmingly believe that character education should be an important part of their curriculum.

This is not surprising. Most teachers chose their professions based on lofty ideals. They wanted to make a difference in the lives of children—to help them become better people.

Sadly, all too often, teachers receive inadequate instruction in character education. This is a grave oversight. Character education is more complex than the teaching skills that we humorously refer to as the three Rs (i.e., reading, writing, arithmetic). It requires addressing personal growth. Therefore, teachers must also be given the proper training to make character education successful and a priority.

The biggest impediment, however, has been legitimizing character education in the curriculum. Beginning in the 1960s, much of the West neglected the importance of character education, instead focusing almost exclusively on the academic basics (e.g., mathematics, reading, etc.). The erosion of our cultural continuity, however, soon became apparent. As a result, there has been an awakened interest in teaching our children core values. In the United States, the Congress and President Bill Clinton formally endorsed character education, reminding schools of the importance of teaching unifying morals.

Communities, however, cannot simply lay the responsibility of instilling moral character in their children on the schools. It is vital that each community determine the values it wants to be taught in its schools. Schools, parents, and the community as a whole must collaborate on the vision, objectives, and approaches regarding the values they want taught.

There is no escaping our own responsibility in seeing to it that our children are taught the meaning of character, i.e., the ability to *know* what is good, to *want* what is good, and to *do* good. We must support our communities' schools in this critical role. It is our duty as loyal citizens. The alternative is an unthinkable future. As U.S. President Theodore Roosevelt warned, "To educate a man in mind and not in morals is to educate a menace to society."

E Pluribus Unum (Out of Many, One)

Loyalty, be it to a person, group, or cause, most typically occurs when we personally identify ourselves with the object of our loyalty. Therefore, if we wish to live in a loyal society, it is imperative that we as a people share a common identity.

Schools play a prominent role in facilitating this shared view. To quote a 1945 Harvard-commissioned study on the objective for education in a free society, "It is impossible to escape the realization that our society, like any society, rests on common beliefs and that a major task of education is to perpetuate them." This is no less true today.

What arguably is different today is the more pronounced challenge of absorbing immigrants with diverse religious and linguistic heritages in virtually every prosperous Western nation. Even in countries like the United States, with a long immigrant tradition, the subject of immigration often results in heated debate.

While diversity clearly enriches humankind—and, in our view, is the strength of the nation—it adds significant challenges to unity. Being part of a larger community demands that we identify ourselves with it. As a result, much of the West finds itself needing to assimilate people of diverse religious and linguistic heritages into cohesive societies. Schools have traditionally been the primary catalyst for creating this unified vision of what it means to belong to a nation—to be American, English, French, etc.

In fact, this is something schools should do. One of the main reasons for the creation of public schools in the United States was the need for civic education. As Fletcher notes, "Generating a sense of common ground and shared national identity are as central to the educational mission as teaching the virtues of fair play and disciplined learning."

The purpose, however, should not be to expunge our differences. Different is good! Rather, the goal must be to respect our differences while still seeing ourselves as one people.

The Need for Heroes

The function of the hero in art is to inspire the reader or spectator to continue in the same spirit from where he, the hero, leaves off.

—John Berger, British author and painter

He was a man without heroes. Few would regard this description as a compliment. None would wish it for an epitaph. It signifies the jaded outlook of a life that has been scarred and lonely. The truth is that we all need heroes—people who inspire us, people who help light the way for us through their own example. And loyal societies also need common heroes.

Our heroes are never as large to us as they are in our childhood. It is at this time we learn to dream of the world that can be, and to see ourselves in that dream. In *The Philosophy of Loyalty*, Harvard professor Josiah Royce persuasively argues the importance of these childhood idealizations to our development of virtuous loyalty:

> There is one contribution which childhood . . . makes to a possible future loyalty . . . the well-known disposition to idealize heroes and adventures, to live an imaginary life, to have ideal comrades, and to dream of possible great enterprises. . . . If I had never been fascinated in childhood by my heroes and by the wonders of life, it is harder to fascinate me later with the call of duty. Loyalty . . . is an idealizing of human life, a communion with invisible aspects of our social existence. Too great literalness in the interpretation of human relations is, therefore, a foe to the development of loyalty.

It is this view that has caused some to advocate that the teaching of history be designed to promote civic loyalty. Most notably, William Galston, former deputy assistant for domestic policy to President Clinton, argues that scientific history should be replaced with a "nobler, moralizing history: a pantheon of heroes who confer legitimacy on central institutions and are worthy of emulation."

As we shall see, this view is not without meaningful debate. But of the need for heroes who fight for noble causes, there can be no doubt. Lonely is the man without heroes. And a community of lonely individuals is no community at all, and certainly not one worthy of loyalty.

The Need for Critical Reflection

Schools have a duty to reflect the values of society. As public institutions, their influence represents the official view of society. A sound education, however, demands that we weigh evidence and accept debate.

In fact, building a sustainable, loyal society actually requires that members of the group be able to think critically. This seems to run counter-intuitive to the need to build common identity to create a community. The key is sustainability.

Communities, like life itself, must adapt and evolve to survive. There will always be forces at play to break communities apart. We have watched the collapse of entire nations played out before our eyes as these societies ultimately broke down into smaller, more homogenous groups because they could no longer share a common vision of themselves.

The forces of disintegration become overpowering when groups in society believe that they are being treated unfairly.

And no matter how homogeneous the society, at some point, there will be members of the group who will feel unfairly treated.

It is only through critical reflection that we can adequately address issues of equity and social justice. Without this, the majority will choose either to be blind to injustice or apologists for it.

But ignoring or excusing injustice doesn't make it go away. It only creates a disenfranchised group within society. Without serious attempts to understand and correct inequity, the threat of secession from the group, whether emotionally or physically, is ever present. With both types of succession, the cost to society as a whole is enormous.

This is a critical reason it is the truly loyal who attempt to change what economist Albert Hirschman calls an "objectionable state of affairs." We tend to forget that evils like slavery, racism, and elitism were the norm for society not so long ago. Change occurred not because it was the natural course of things, but because loyal citizens critically considered the issues and challenged conventional wisdom.

Therefore, schools must not only provide our children with knowledge; they must teach them the critical thinking skills necessary to handle the complex issues that come with maturity. Only in this way will citizens have the capacity for loyally opposing the status quo when the will of the majority actually threatens the sustainability of the community.

And it is only through critical thinking that the majority will see the value in such thinking.

Reconciling the Need for Heroes and Critical Thinking

Florida State University philosophy professor Victoria Costa argues, "educational systems can promote . . . two sorts of goals. One such goal is the production of citizens who are loyal to a particular community. Another . . . is the development of a student's capabilities for rational inquiry directed at the pursuit of truth . . . there is a clear tension between these two goals."

Without question, Professor Costa is correct. But it is also true that these two goals, loyal citizenship and critical reflection, are not mutually exclusive. As Martin Luther King Jr. eloquently argued:

> Education must enable one to sift and weigh evidence, to discern the true from the false, the real from the unreal, and the facts from the fiction. The function of education, therefore, is to teach one to think intensively and to think critically. But education which stops with efficiency may prove the greatest menace to society. The most dangerous criminal may be the man gifted with reason, but with no morals. . . . We must remember that intelligence is not enough. Intelligence plus character—that is the goal of true education.

The fact is that we need to provide our children with heroes *and* critical thinking in their education. Unfortunately, the debate seems to be between the extremes on both sides.

Free societies are legitimately mindful of their past— visions of "Hitler Youth" indoctrinations cannot, and should not, be forgotten. Similarly, we are wary of the sometimes-deadly fanaticism inculcated on impressionable youth in some schools in countries around the world today.

On the other hand, educators sometimes overemphasize the negative in our past, to a point that seemingly takes the position that history will teach us nothing except that mankind has suffered over the ages at the hands of various power-hungry despots.

Without question, history is filled with lessons in suffering. And all regimes of any size and longevity have committed acts that violate the rights we now believe inalienable to all of humankind. But the truth is also that life for the human race has never been better than it is at this very moment. And this did not happen by accident. It is the direct result of the sacrifices of many heroes of our past, without whom our ability to pursue happiness would be unimaginable. Those who advocate a completely airbrushed view of our heroes do a tremendous disservice to both our heroes and to the citizens they seek to impress. Infallibility should be left to religious avatars. By removing our heroes from the self-doubts and failings common to all of humanity, their self-sacrifice for the betterment of humankind is reduced to the preordained fate of supermen and superwomen. The message to our youth becomes not simply that these individuals are great, but that they are nothing like us. If they are nothing like us, then the fate of the world is someone else's problem, or worse still, unfixable by the people of today. Our heroes need to be inspirational and aspirational—otherwise, our best days will always be behind us.

Those who advocate an unvarnished view of our heroes do no less a disservice to our heroes and our citizens. All of us, no matter how great our achievements, have significant failings. Were our lives to be the sum of our failings and foibles, all of us would leave legacies of shame. Unfortunately, what is often put forth as critical thinking is in fact cynical thinking—focusing on the failings of the heroes of our past rather than highlighting their accomplishments.

For example, George Washington, the leader of the patriot forces in the American Revolutionary War and the first president of the United States, made extraordinary sacrifices in the service of creating the nation. He also owned slaves. Without question, slavery represents a great evil. Of this there can be no debate. Given all that George Washington sacrificed and accomplished to establish the United States, however, was he not a great man—a hero who should be admired by American citizens? Those who would answer that his ownership of slaves disqualifies him from being regarded as a hero stand atop a steep and slippery slope. Just how steep and how slippery will become readily apparent.

The Jewish, Christian, and Islamic faiths all share a common patriarch, Abraham. Abraham is believed by the faithful to be the forefather of the Jewish and Arab peoples, and to have had a direct dialogue with God. The sacred texts of these faiths also reveal that Abraham owned slaves. In fact, he had a child with one of these slaves. To those who practice what we have labeled as cynical thinking, are the two billion plus Jews, Christians, and Muslims to repudiate their patriarch and abandon their faith over Abraham's ownership of slaves? The answer is self-evident. Regardless of our belief or lack thereof in these faiths, the idea that Abraham's ownership of slaves disqualifies the admiration of Jews, Christians, and Muslims toward him is absurd.

The key in resolving the need for heroes and the need for critical thinking is "balanced" education. We are reminded of a eulogy given for Bruce Henderson, the founder of the Boston Consulting Group, whose contributions to the science and practice of management are still strongly felt today.

> He was not always easy to deal with. My vivid recollection of those early days is that periodically some brilliant young person would come into my office and say, "Do you know what he did to me?" It was never necessary to ask to whom they were referring. I responded to each in the same way: "Look, don't think of Bruce as an ordinary

person—Bruce is a great man. Neither his virtues nor his failings are small. Fortunately, his virtues outweigh his failings or neither of us would be here."

So it is with all great men and women. Like us, they are filled with virtues and failings. Thankfully, most of us will leave this life with our virtues outweighing our failings. Our heroes simply do so in greater magnitude. This is what we must teach to our children, and constantly remind ourselves.

It is not simply our heroes' strength of courage that should give us comfort but their own human frailties. It is their frailties that prove to us all that our weaknesses do not disqualify us from achieving great things. We all can be heroes if we are willing to commit ourselves to noble causes. This represents the pinnacle of loyalty—the devotion of a person to a cause that unites many as one. This is the underlying quality of our heroes. This is why loyalty ultimately matters. And it is attainable by us all.

Chapter 8

A Loyal Society

Until philosophers are kings . . . cities will never have rest from their troubles.

—Plato, *The Republic*, Commonwealth, Book V

My Role in a Loyal Society

The past 400 years have brought the most profound shift in how we view the world and our place in it. Science has unrelentingly diminished the importance of our home planet in relation to the universe. Our ancient forefathers could look to the sky convinced of one thing—the Earth was the center of the universe. With Galileo, Earth was relegated to being the third planet in the solar system in what was believed to be the Milky Way "universe." And following the discoveries of Edwin Hubble in the twentieth century, Earth became just one of perhaps an infinite number of planets orbiting stars in a seemingly infinite number of galaxies.

Paradoxically, as our perception of our world in relation to the universe has shrunk to an almost infinitesimally small speck, our view of the importance of the individual has expanded on a virtually unbounded scale. In the twenty-first century, individual rights reign supreme. Independence is the goal of virtually every adult. And expressing our individuality defines our self-image.

We have taken our belief in the importance of the individual to its pinnacle. Of course, every one of us is indeed important. We all matter! And while some organizations classify select individuals as VIPs, the reality is that we are all Very Important People!

Clearly, there is nothing wrong with seeing ourselves as valuable. We are! But there is a tremendous difference between self-worth and self-absorption. Narcissism causes us to devalue loyalty, unless we conveniently define supreme loyalty as being loyal to oneself. As philosophy professor Donald De Marco argues, "If you're saying the highest loyalty is to self, you can't get beyond self. Therefore, you're missing an essential element of loyalty. It's not a virtue to be loyal to oneself."

No man is an island. Virtually all of us live in communities. All but a handful of us have strong communal ties. So no matter how strongly individualistic our viewpoint may be, we exist as part of a larger social organism. Distinguished University of Chicago professor John Cacioppo notes, "the need for meaningful social connection, and the pain we feel without it, are defining characteristics of our species."

Whether our personal philosophies place emphasis on social cohesion or individual liberties, living in a free society demands that we manage to achieve both simultaneously. Philosophers have long debated the merits of individualism versus collectivism and all points along the continuum between the two. But while these concepts—individualism and collectivism—are clearly distinct perspectives unto themselves, they do not have to conflict with one another. Sociologist Amitai Etzioni observes, "One and all will recognize the merit of autonomy . . . [as well as] the need for some measure of social order . . . and a carefully crafted balance between the two."

For us as individuals, it is vital that we remember that every dream we hope to achieve in this life is going to be accomplished through our relationships with others. We really cannot get anywhere alone. As nineteenth-century columnist George Matthew Adams writes, "There is no such thing as a 'self-made' man. We are made up of thousands of others. Everyone who has ever done a kind deed for us, or spoken one word of encouragement to us, has entered into the make-up of our character and of our thoughts, as well as our success."

Most of us recognize this. But what we often fail to see is that our individual acts of loyalty to members of our community actually impact the kind of communities we have. In his book *Loneliness*, Professor Cacioppo persuasively presents evidence that making seemingly minor positive connections with others dramatically alters our happiness and the happiness of those with whom we connect, and alters the communities in which we live.

In many ways, we are all George Bailey, the character Jimmy Stewart played in the classic movie *It's a Wonderful Life*. In the movie, an angel shows a broken and suicidal Bailey what life in his small town would have been like had he never existed. In this alternate reality, Bailey's hometown of Bedford Falls is nightmarishly transformed. The people he touched and those he loved live a dejected existence—some have even died. The lesson for George Bailey was that the cumulative effect of his loyalty to his family, friends, and the community at large dramatically altered the course of history in Bedford Falls. George Bailey did indeed have a wonderful life, and he helped to create one for others.

While this obviously is just a movie, the fundamental message is no less real. What we do in this life matters. Our individual behaviors continuously modify our social environment. Yes, there are large forces at work (economic, political, etc.), but we are not powerless. As Professor Cacioppo notes, "each of us has a certain degree of power, through our individual actions, to continuously adjust the social environment toward something slightly better or something slightly worse."

Therefore, given that each of us has this power, then each of us bears the responsibility to act in way that guides our social environment toward something better. It is our duty as loyal members of our communities.

Yes, our rights as individuals are unassailable. But our responsibility to foster a better world is no less significant.

The good news is that this simple philosophy actually benefits us. Research conclusively shows that we get an emotional high from helping others that lasts long after the helping is done. And our research clearly shows that our level of involvement with our communities leads to far greater satisfaction with our lives.

Life Satisfaction by Community Involvement

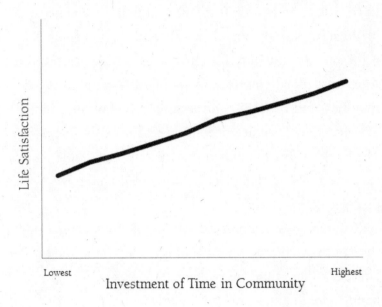

Lowest   Highest

Investment of Time in Community

Source: Ipsos Loyalty

These acts of loyalty don't have to be grand gestures—in fact, they almost never are. Simply demonstrating that we all are indeed important by seeking to make a connection with others—no matter how informal or brief—through simple acts of kindness and consideration ultimately has a profound impact on our communities and ourselves. Given the small effort to obtain such a large return, we are all without a doubt up to the task. We simply have to be willing to take up the task.

The Media's Role in a Loyal Society

In the late twentieth century, the traditional social networks of Western society visibly weakened. In his book *Bowling Alone*, Robert Putnam chronicles the deterioration of American social connections—to family, neighbors, communities, and country—in the second half of the twentieth century. Our lives are becoming less socially interactive. The book's title exemplified this observation: "More Americans are bowling than ever before, but league bowling has plummeted."

Putnam lays much of the fraying of our social fabric on the "individualizing" nature of our electronic media. He laments, "Electronic technology allows us to consume this hand-tailored entertainment in private, even utterly alone. As late as the middle of the twentieth century, low-cost entertainment was available primarily in public settings, like the baseball park, the dance hall, the movie theater, and the amusement park . . . As the poet T.S. Eliot observed early in the television age, 'It is a medium of entertainment which permits millions of people to listen to the same joke at the same time, and yet remain lonesome.'"

There is no question that we now have tremendous opportunities to be both connected to others via electronic media, yet remain completely anonymous and unaccompanied. We can even build synthetic identities, complete with virtual wives, jobs, and mortgages. As the real living, breathing wife of a cyberholic laments, "This other life is so wonderful; it's better than real life. Nobody gets fat, nobody gets gray. The person that's left can't compete with that." If only it were real!

Fortunately, most of us know the boundary between the virtual world and reality. But our ability to satisfy our own distinct appetites has led to increasing fragmentation of our personal lives. A study by Deloitte reports, "In recent years, the number of media formats and channels has exploded—changing the way people consume content and splintering the mass market into smaller pieces . . . that translates into a fragmented world of increasingly scattered audiences."

Furthermore, this fragmentation abets asocial ideas. The ability of the media to provide subject matter on virtually any idea means there is ready access to content for the lunatic fringe of society. A study conducted by the New York City Police Department states, "The Internet is a driver and enabler for the process of radicalization . . . It also serves as an anonymous virtual meeting place—a place where virtual groups of like-minded and conflicted individuals can meet, form virtual relationships and discuss and share the . . . message they have encountered."

Whether or not the decline in social networks is primarily attributable to the individualizing aspects of modern electronic media is clearly debatable. But let's assume for the moment that it is. Should we give up our iPod, our satellite TV and radio, our Internet access to live in a more cohesive society, where loyalty to other citizens is as obvious as it is fulfilling? For many (if not most) of us, the idea of moving backward to a technologically simpler era sounds too severe an action to bear.

But we should realize that if we don't moderate the effects of our electronic entanglements, we put at risk our most basic and common humanity. There is a definite connection between our level of personal interaction and our social selves as citizens. Alexis de Tocqueville's observations more than 150 years ago still ring true:

> When men are no longer united in any firm or lasting way, it is impossible to persuade any great number of them to act in cooperation unless you convince each of those whose help is vital that his private interests are served by voluntarily joining his efforts to those of all the others. This cannot be achieved usually or conveniently except with the help of a newspaper, which is the only way of being able to place the same thought at the same moment into a thousand minds.

De Tocqueville reminds us that civic loyalty was once tied to the news we received from our media. Unfortunately, modern news is often driven by the ratings it will generate, filtered by political ideology, and narrowly broadcast to like-minded constituents. So instead of producing the "same thought at the same moment into a thousand minds," we now transmit different thoughts at the same moment targeted to those who already believe. We no longer interact with the community at large but only with those portions of the community with which we agree.

The Founding Fathers of the United States believed strongly that free societies required a free press. Thomas Jefferson famously said, "Were it left to me to decide whether we should have a government without newspapers or newspapers without a government, I should not hesitate a moment to prefer the latter." But Jefferson also added, "But I should mean that every man should receive those papers and be capable of reading them."

The First Amendment grants freedom of the press in the United States. And while all countries do not provide constitutional protection to the press, Western countries provide news organizations with great latitude so that reporters are able to uncover and report the truth. But with every right comes a responsibility. The free press is supposed to remain loyal to the people. This requires offering the public a forum for open, honest political discourse.

Hence, it is ironic that parody news programs—namely *The Daily Show* and *The Colbert Report*—are viewed by many Americans (specifically Americans under the age of forty-five) as truly honoring the media's duty. A key responsibility of the press is to challenge truthiness with the truth. (*Truthiness* is a term that Stephen Colbert, faux-conservative anchor of *The Colbert Report*, popularized, defined as "the quality of preferring concepts or facts one wishes to be true, rather than concepts or facts known to be true.") In an out-of-persona interview, Colbert laments:

> Truthiness is tearing apart our country . . . it doesn't seem to matter what facts are. It used to be [that] everyone was entitled to their own opinion, but not their own facts. But that's not the case anymore. Facts matter not at all. Perception is everything. It's certainty. . . . What is important? What you want to be true, or what is true?

So what part of the equation has changed? Why do we find that people are willing to accept gut instinct over verifiable truth? Well, this type of skewed media has always been available. But nowadays, intellectually honest debate is sorely lacking. Debates in the news are choreographed and the true essence of debate is spoiled. Often, conservative and liberal representatives merely repeat the party line so that they simply talk past one another without listening to or addressing the legitimate concerns of citizens. So, perhaps it is the fleeting concept of open and public discourse that allows the proliferation of "truthiness" to go unchecked.

To quote Jefferson again,

> No experiment can be more interesting than that we are now trying, and which we trust will end in establishing the fact, that man may be governed by reason and truth. Our first object should therefore be, to leave open

to him all the avenues to truth. The most effectual hith-
erto found, is the freedom of the press.

In other words, Jefferson believed that the press is the
primary means of ensuring our liberty. And, as de Tocqueville observed, it is also the primary means of ensuring
our loyalty to our communities while maintaining our individual rights.

Therefore, the press must exercise its great power to
bring honest discourse to the people, recognizing its vital
role in maintaining liberty, and fostering civic loyalty. And it
should do so with vigor.

Government's Role in a Loyal Society

May 1 is a legal holiday in the United States: Loyalty Day.
Interestingly, most Americans are unaware of it.

Loyalty Day began in 1921 as "Americanization Day" in
response to the communists' celebration of the Russian Revolution. In 1958, the U.S. Congress made Loyalty Day an
official holiday and every American president since Dwight
D. Eisenhower—except for Richard Nixon, ironically—has
issued a Loyalty Day proclamation at some point during his
administration. And though this holiday has been trum-
peted by presidents, the rest of America seldom observes it.
Nonetheless, regardless of political affiliation or ideology,
American presidents consistently regard the formal affirma-
tion of our national loyalty to be a good thing.

Recognizing the importance of loyalty to the continued strength of our country and success of our democracy, the Congress . . . has designated May 1 of each year as "Loyalty Day." I urge all Americans to recall the valor and selflessness of all those who made this Nation worthy of our love and loyalty and to express our own loyalty through appropriate patriotic programs, ceremonies, and activities.

—William Jefferson Clinton, forty-second
president of the United States

For nearly 30 years, Americans have celebrated May 1 as Loyalty Day. This is a day to reaffirm our loyalty to our land of liberty and to recall with pride and gratitude the generations of our countrymen who preserved our freedom by their loyalty to America. Loyalty to our country means being faithful to our heritage of liberty and justice for all.

—Ronald Reagan, fortieth president
of the United States

Although some regard the idea of a Loyalty Day to be more comical than inspiring, most Americans regard themselves as loyal to their country. But such loyalty is far from unique. Billions of Earth's citizenry consider themselves as having fierce loyalty to their country—we intentionally distinguish here between *country* and *government*.

The concept of *country* extends far beyond simple territory. Country is comprised of its people, their ideals, their culture, and their way of life. This concept is often a vision within the heart of each citizen, how they view the greater sense of their own country. The concept of *government* is simply the group of folks (usually) elected to guide the practices of a given nation toward its ideal form.

But as the American Revolution demonstrates, loyalty to country and loyalty to government are not the same things. The Founding Fathers of the United States were willing to risk all for their unborn country, yet they loathed the British monarchy to which they were subjected. Therefore, it is as American author Mark Twain insisted, "Loyalty to the country always, loyalty to the government when it deserves it."

Twain draws attention to one of the most clear and profound principles in the U.S. Declaration of Independence— legitimate governments derive their powers from the consent of the governed. And consent to such a government is only offered when citizens are "created equal" and afforded the opportunity to secure their rights to "life, liberty, and the pursuit of happiness." Herein lies the ultimate responsibility of any government that seeks to secure the loyalty (as opposed to obedience) of its people:

- "Equal laws protecting equal rights . . . the best guarantee of loyalty & love of country."—James Madison, fourth president of the United States
- "The happiness of society is the end [goal] of government. . . . From this principle it will follow that the form of government which communicates ease,

comfort, security, or, in one word, happiness to the greatest number of persons, and in the greatest degree, is the best."—John Adams, second president of the United States

Government has a duty to be bound, to be loyal to the citizens from whom it derives its legitimate powers. While much has been written about the duty of government to its people, it would be difficult to find a more eloquent summary than John F. Kennedy's monologue on the standards by which political leaders must be measured:

When at some future date the high court of history sits in judgment on each of us—recording whether in our brief span of service we fulfilled our responsibilities to the state—our success or failure, in whatever office we hold, will be measured by the answers to four questions:

First, were we truly men of courage—with the courage to stand up to one's enemies—and the courage to stand up, when necessary, to one's associates—the courage to resist public pressure, as well as private greed?

Secondly, were we truly men of judgment—with perceptive judgment of the future as well as the past—of our mistakes as well as the mistakes of others—with enough wisdom to know what we did not know and enough candor to admit it?

Third, were we truly men of integrity—men who never ran out on either the principles in which we believed or the men who believed in us—men whom neither financial gain nor political ambition could ever divert from the fulfillment of our sacred trust?

Finally, were we truly men of dedication—with an honor mortgaged to no single individual or group, and comprised of no private obligation or aim, but devoted solely to serving the public good and the national interest?

Kennedy powerfully summarized what is expected of our elected officials. All politicians inherently know that this is what is expected of them when they choose public service. As such, adherence to these standards is the criterion for determining the loyalty of our political leaders to the people that they have sworn to serve.

Too often, citizens find themselves jaded by the failings of our governments. But they are *our* governments. While a government that meets its duty of loyalty to the people may sound like the ideal, it is not. It is merely the minimally acceptable threshold of government. Our loyalty to our country requires it. And it is our national and patriotic duty of loyalty to insist on nothing less.

Awakening

In the religious texts and mythologies of many cultures, humankind was thought to have once lived a utopian existence: a world without war, where all needs were met, and where man existed in harmony with nature. But at some point, paradise was lost. The Judeo–Christian–Muslim traditions declare that our failings as humans ultimately caused our expulsion from this Eden.

But our desire for an ideal society never ceases. Many of our greatest minds have pondered how we should live. This is the cornerstone of philosophy and ethics.

In Plato's *Republic*, Socrates contemplates the perfect society, ultimately concluding that until the people are ruled by philosopher–kings, our societies will always have problems.

So how does loyalty fit within this vision of a perfect society? Plato believed that only honorable people could be loyal, and that loyalty was a necessary component of genuine philosophy.

More important than philosophical perspective of loyalty in society, however, are the practical implications. The vitality of any society is dependent upon the civic mindedness of its citizens. As such, loyalty is the foundation of any cohesive community. Therefore, the breaking of our bonds with one another has serious ramifications for the whole of society.

Few would argue with the notion that some of the most pressing problems facing society have been exacerbated by a breakdown in our connections with one another. The isolation that many feel in our increasingly atomized culture brings with it a host of problems.

At its most extreme, a sense of loneliness and isolation contributes to resentment against society. This anger makes it even harder to build close, loyal relationships. Sadly, in extremely rare cases, this resentment even boils over, contributing to horrific acts committed against society at large.

Of course, the overwhelming majority of socially isolated people do not become sociopaths. But without question, a sense of isolation causes suffering: impaired sleep, depression, alcoholism, and in some cases, even suicide.

And even if none of the above applies to the majority of society, social isolation causes our bodies to take a beating. Research has found that lonely people have lower-functioning immune systems. It also causes our bodies to age faster—at least on the inside.

The economic consequences to society are staggering. If the cause of these costs to our health and happiness were the result of a contaminant in our air or water—instead of a result of a decline in loyalty—the public would demand action by their governments, and stigmatize individual behaviors that contribute to the pollution. Given the consequences, we need to treat the decline in loyalty equally seriously. As Professor Cacioppo writes:

> Perhaps we can hope for [an] awakening to the idea, grounded in rigorous science, that restoring bonds among people can be a cost-effective and practical point of leverage for solving some of our most pressing social

problems, not the least of which is the looming crisis in health care and eldercare.

When we think about the *why* of a loyal society, this is the end result of the bargain. We can improve our communities and our own lives by building positive bonds with one another through friends and family, education, faith, and government, to name a few. This is our collective social voice. But doing this demands that we make our duty to one another a meaningful social priority again.

Our loyalty is about far more than practical or selfish self-preservation. It is about being human. It is about ensuring our *social health* in an effort to foster our own *emotional* and *physical health*. And building and maintaining this social loyalty is the responsibility of us all: our governments, our press, our institutions, and most importantly, our fellow citizens. This is what makes us secure. And this is the best means to life, liberty, and the pursuit of happiness.

Chapter 9

Enlightened Loyalty

Our loyalties must transcend our race, our tribe, our class, and our nation.

—Martin Luther King Jr.

A Loyal Life

The most valuable thing that can be given to any person, entity, or cause is not money. It is you! There is nothing more powerful than the human will, nothing more precious than the human spirit. Through our loyalty, we literally invest that will and spirit to create something greater than we can achieve alone.

As such, our loyalties are signs of the types of people we choose to be. They are the foundation of our character. Our loyalties demonstrate what we value, what we believe, and what we want our world to be. But like any aspect of character, real loyalty sometimes requires sacrifice. As former U.S. Secretary of Education William Bennett observes, "Real loyalty endures inconvenience, withstands temptation, and does not cringe under assault."

Loyalty requires deliberate effort, constant practice, and conscious employment. American political consultant James Carville asks, "What do you do in your everyday life? What do you choose to be loyal to every day?"

Few of us give serious consideration to such questions. Instead, we let the frenetic pace of our everyday lives eat away at the loyalties that connect us to one another.

Yet without a conscious effort to build bonds with others, loyalty doesn't just happen. We are not born loyal. Loyalty is not instinctive. Instead, we must learn to be loyal. Being loyal is the manifestation of the choices we make in life. And we choose our loyalties each and every day, even though we seldom recognize them as such. These are the decisions that influence and reflect our desire to stay in a relationship, whatever that relationship might be.

A handful of these decisions are monumental. Most of them are not. These choices represent the hundreds of things we faithfully do each day. Without them, our world would not function.

While these decisions in loyalty seem inconsequential in and of themselves, taken as a whole, they are extremely important. We train ourselves in the art of loyalty through them. And for the world at large, it is the small yet numerous acts of loyalty or disloyalty that help determine the kind of communities in which we live.

Therefore, if loyalty is to be an important part of our lives, then we must become aware of the ramifications of our decisions. Living a loyal life requires that we recognize the formal and implicit commitments we have made to others. We must then make deliberate choices to strengthen our bonds by honoring our commitments.

Of course, it's easy to turn this idea into little more than a platitude—"be good to one another"—instead of a practical approach for building loyal connections with others. To help transform this philosophy into a tangible approach to living, we recommend following what we refer to as the P_2R_2 process. No, this isn't one of the robots in the Star Wars series . . . at least not one of which we are aware. P_2R_2 stands for *Pinpoint, Prioritize, Reinforce,* and *Reach Out.*

The P_2R_2 Process

P_1 IS FOR *PINPOINT WHERE YOU ARE*

While traveling in San Francisco recently, we found ourselves completely lost immediately after we left the airport in our rental car. We had hoped to prevent just such an occurrence by bringing along our GPS from home. But when we programmed in the address, the turn-by-turn directions made absolutely no sense. The mileage was astronomical, and the time for arrival at our destination was best measured in days. Because the GPS unit could not locate the satellites it used to mark its position, it used the last known location. Unfortunately for us, that was on the other side of the continent. After twenty minutes had gone by with no satellite link, we gave up hope that we would get meaningful directions soon, got directions to a restaurant from a kind stranger, parked the car, and waited out the time until the

GPS realized that this was San Francisco, not the suburbs of New York City.

The reality is that it's hard to get where you want to go if you don't know where you are. The same is true for strengthening our loyalties. Typically, we believe we are far more loyal than the recipients of our loyalty believe us to be.

The LoyaltyAdvisor assessment included with this book provides an evaluation of how you view your loyalties, and how your friends and family view them. Knowing this information is an important first step toward improving your bonds with others.

Once you have digested the information from your LoyaltyAdvisor assessment, it's important to reflect on your most loyal relationships: the things, causes, and people to whom you are most loyal. Take the time to write these down, thinking in particular about the following:

- What relationships are you currently invested in?
- Who do you consistently connect with?
- What organizations do you feel a strong sense of loyalty toward?
- Which causes hold special significance to you?

For most of this, doing this simple exercise hammers home just how large a role loyalties play in our lives. It becomes even more compelling when we realize that these represent only those loyalties that hold a strong place in our lives. Virtually all of us have numerous other connections that we believe to be part of the fabric of our lives.

For many of us, actually putting into words what it is that we hold dear causes us to consider how well we have actually done in demonstrating our loyalties. Sometimes, we find ourselves thinking that we've failed those that matter to us. The point of this exercise, however, is not to make us feel down. None of us can change our past, but we all have a say in our future. And now that we are clear on whom and what we believe really deserves our strongest loyalty, we can act in a way that proves our beliefs.

P₂ IS FOR *PRIORITIZE THOSE THINGS THAT MATTER*

Science and technology have allowed us to become more productive than ever. The number of hours we work each week has declined significantly over the last 200 years. So why is it that we always feel like we're working, like we're always running behind?

For one thing, despite the decline in work hours, we still spend a significant part of our time working. Most of us spend a third or more of our waking hours on average either doing work or compulsory activities.

The bulk of the remainder of our days, however, tends to be spent doing very little—what is referred to as "passive leisure." These are activities that don't require us to connect with others and require little, if any, intellectual stimulation, such as watching television.

We spend only a tiny fraction of our days in active leisure—activities that tend to require that we connect with others. As a point of comparison, the amount of time is roughly equivalent to the amount of time we spend eating.

Given the way many of us spend our discretionary time, our loyalties are bound to be strained as a consequence. Loyalty is about connecting with others. And connecting with others requires making time for that actually to happen.

We all have rhetorically asked, "Where has the time gone?" But if we want to make loyalty a meaningful part of our everyday existence, then we need to understand where we are actually spending our time.

This sounds like a fairly simple exercise, but the reality is that it is quite hard. Take the time to outline how you spend your time, and with whom you spend it, in a given month. How much time do you spend:

- At work?
- With your family?
- With your friends?
- Working for causes you believe in?
- Doing basically nothing?

How much time goes to things that inevitably hurt you, worsening your perspective, or ruining your day? How much of what you do with your time actually leaves you feeling uplifted and strong?

Once we know where we currently allocate our time, we need to consider how and where we would *prefer* to be spending our time. Think back to those important loyalties in your life that you pinpointed earlier. How much of your time is actually allocated to maintaining these bonds?

Of course, we all have certain obligations that we must do: work, shopping for groceries, driving our children to piano lessons, and other compulsory activities. And without question, a move, a new job, a new school, etc. all can make it difficult to maintain important connections in our lives.

But the issue isn't having it all—it's having more of it. There will always be things that compete for our time. Some will be compulsory activities. Some will even be competing loyalties. Ironically, we frequently choose to spend our time doing things that will not make us happier instead of connecting with those who fill us up emotionally.

When thinking about how we should allocate our time, we need to remember this simple saying, "How do you spell love? T-I-M-E." Loyalty is spelled the same way.

Doing this requires that we set priorities and make a serious effort to maintain our connection with those people and things to which we feel most loyal. If we don't make time to care for the bonds we cherish in our lives, then these relationships can wither and die.

Often we lament, "Life gets in the way" when we have crowded out the things that give our lives meaning. But if we are honest with ourselves, most of the time the truth is "Our priorities were wrong."

R₁ IS FOR *REINFORCE YOUR CONNECTIONS*

One of the great things about being human is our capacity to love. In fact, our wide-ranging ability to love has caused us to ascribe the word *love* to things that appear odd when considering that this is the word we use to describe our strongest positive feelings for our mate, our children, and our country. Yet we often hear (and say) things like, "I love . . . pizza, my car, those earrings, sunny days, walks in the park, New York, sleeping late," just to name a few.

Strangely, other than family members, most of us rarely if ever tell those to whom we feel most connected that we love them. Given the importance of these individuals to our happiness, this doesn't make much sense. We need to tell these people how we feel about having them in our lives (even if we don't feel comfortable using the word *love*), and specifically state how it is that we benefit from owning a relationship with them.

Make a verbal commitment to them that you will try to honor that relationship and not overlook it. This sounds corny, but it is the kind of thing that anyone deserving of your loyalty will appreciate.

Remember that it's not enough simply to make the commitment to honor your relationship. You actually have to do it! Consider ways in which you can positively reinforce the relationship. Recognize the efforts that the other person makes on your behalf and then reciprocate. Healthy loyalty is the give-and-take that spawns reverence for one another!

This will involve simple things like keeping promises, honoring confidences, being considerate, and being available. But most of all, it will mean that there will be times we must sacrifice doing things that would be more fun to help a friend in need. Know that if someone to whom you have pledged your loyalty says (or you can see) that he or she really needs you that you have vowed to make yourself eligible to help in any *positive* way that you can. It is this aspect of loyalty that we cherish most. It keeps us all secure!

Most of us tend to think that we already do these things anyway. And we might actually do so if we were immersed and active in our relationships. But the reality is that these acts of loyalty rarely happen if we haven't made the effort to keep these connections vibrant. So perhaps the most important step in reinforcing our loyalties is to actively schedule time to connect with those to whom we owe loyalty.

R_2 IS FOR *REACH OUT TO OTHERS*

Before you started reading this book, you probably never had a categorical vision of loyalty: its importance, its timelessness, its breadth. Seldom, if ever, do we ever consider the intertwined nature that loyalty has shared with the coinciding success of humanity. Did you ever picture the functioning of our society as incumbent on this often-overlooked pillar of the human experience? Probably not.

Just like you (before reading this book), most of your friends and neighbors don't think about loyalty in an everyday sense either. But this is where the crux of loyalty's power resides—the actions of the empowered. By reading this book, you have dedicated some time to the pursuit of loyalty, learning about it, and how to make it better. But its greatest contribution to humanity comes from understanding the power and the potential of loyalty to strengthen the ties that bind communities and society at large together.

The good news is that there will never be a better person to change your day-to-day world than you. But unleashing this power requires that we extend our own loyalty to some entity or to some other person so that the flame from our candle metaphorically lights the way for others to see the value of loyalty.

Think you can't do it? It sounds daunting. But the truth is that we're not talking about grand acts of loyalty. We're not asking you to force upheaval onto a society ripe for change. We're asking you to engage in a better way of change. In fact, it usually starts out small.

Begin by starting with what you know. Take your existing loyalties and invest in them even more. And then demonstrate that investment to the world.

If you believe something is important to the vitality of your community, then become a part of the solution. Give of yourself in some way. Then help others to get involved. For example, if you believe strongly that education is the critical path to self-empowerment and social justice, then find a way to help children learn. As Gandhi said, "Be the change you wish to see in the world." This is the essence of reaching out.

Most of the leading thinkers in science and personal development recognize the imperative of reaching out to our own happiness. Professor John Cacioppo, past president of the Association for Psychological Science, finds failing to connect with our community leads to feelings of loneliness, regardless of our connection with romantic partners and close friends. Similarly, Anthony Robbins makes clear to his audiences that having all the positive thinking, security, stimulation, success, or even love in the world will not leave you fulfilled: "Fulfillment only comes when we give of ourselves to others."

Clearly, engage your friends and family. But also engage your neighbors. It will make a better "little world" for you and your neighbors. And stay with it. By continuing to reach out, eventually the realm of the little world gets a bit bigger.

Our actions demonstrate that loyalty matters. Letting others see that we are engaged reminds our neighbors that we live in a place where a sense of loyalty and belonging is something that we honor. It fulfills the promise of loyalty.

It says, this relationship, this institution, this cause is *mine*, and I will not abandon it.

In the end, we can find many things to do that stretch our existing loyalties to include others. Ultimately, this must be what loyalty is about. And isn't that the whole point—gaining the reverence and respect that allow us to develop a more thoughtful, deliberate, and meaningful way of interacting with one another?

It All Matters

Although each of us is unique, at our core, we all want the same things: to be happy, to be fulfilled, and to be loved. Moreover, each of us longs for a better world. We fail to recognize, however, that this wish for our own happiness and for a more humane world rests on the same foundation: our loyalty to one another.

But loyalty doesn't just happen. Being loyal is a deliberate act. There are no accidental loyalties. We must take an active role.

Making loyalty a driving force in your life is never an easy road. Often, we only see the potential hazards. We become exposed, risking rejection and betrayal. But to quote American author Erica Jong, "If you don't risk anything, you risk even more."

We must overcome our fear of rejection, be open to new connections, and be willing to forgive when we are at times let down. By doing so, we can amplify the quality of our lives through the joy that can only come from having friends, family, co-workers, and others who are willing to bond with us and who are willing to put themselves at risk emotionally for us in order to be a part of our lives in a positive and meaningful way.

These reciprocal, loyal, loving relationships fill us with positive emotions. Although they don't eliminate negative experiences from our lives, they provide us with a wellspring of positive experiences to drown the negative. This is what makes for lasting happiness.

And it is the collective of these positive, loyal connections that make for strong communities. This is true not only for our local communities but for our nation, and for the community of nations.

Loyalty is the raw material of every human value and institution. While it seems idealistic to believe that what we as individuals do in our everyday life can tangibly alter the world in which we live, it actually can and does.

So we can either choose to lament the state of loyalty in our personal lives, in our communities, and in society at large, or we can actively work to create the world in which we wish to live. We have everything to gain. We have everything to lose. It is ours to choose.

You may never know what results come of your action, but if you do nothing there will be no result.

—Mahatma Gandhi

A Technical Supplement to LoyaltyAdvisor

Alexander Buoye and Howard Lyeth
in conjunction with the authors, Timothy Keiningham,
Lerzan Aksoy, and Luke Williams

Your purchase of *Why Loyalty Matters* includes one-time access to the accompanying online LoyaltyAdvisor™ tool. To take the LoyaltyAdvisor assessment, log onto the Internet and enter this URL: *http://www.loyaltyadvisor.com*. You will be prompted to enter a unique access code, which is located on the reverse side of the dust jacket of this book.

Have you completed it yet?

You may be curious about how LoyaltyAdvisor was designed and how it works. In this technical appendix, we will go behind the scenes to give you some general information about the process behind this tool. In the reference section, we have included a brief list of readings for readers who would like to delve deeper into the issues discussed.

However, LoyaltyAdvisor will be useful to you only to the extent that you are honest with yourself and reflect that honesty in your answers. After all, remember that there are no right or wrong answers!

What Is LoyaltyAdvisor?

LoyaltyAdvisor is an online assessment tool that asks a series of questions about how we view ourselves, our interactions with others, and the level to which we find ourselves loyal to others. It is designed to help individuals know themselves better.

In turn, LoyaltyAdvisor generates a report based on the given responses, which are aimed at helping individuals understand the way they relate to other people in terms of their relationship styles, how they deal with problems in their lives, and to what degree they perceive themselves as loyal to their friends, family, and society in general.

LoyaltyAdvisor allows you to compare your relationship style and loyalty level to the top 15 percent of individuals in terms of life satisfaction. The purpose is to help you recognize aspects of your relationship styles and loyalties that have the potential to have either a positive or negative impact on your happiness.

The LoyaltyAdvisor tool also provides you with the opportunity to have your friends and family assess your loyalty to them. Because we know that the perceptions of one's family and friends are likely to differ from one's own, we strongly encourage you to take advantage of this opportunity to see yourself through the eyes of others. LoyaltyAdvisor allows up to ten of your friends and family members to provide feedback.

With insight into where you stand on these various issues, you can use this information to adapt certain aspects of the way you approach situations, ultimately to be happier in life and to be more fulfilled!

What Is the Theoretical Grounding Behind LoyaltyAdvisor?

Before we designed LoyaltyAdvisor, we conducted a thorough review of previous research as documented in the literature of psychology, organizational behavior, management, and marketing. The objective was to make sure that the tool we devised was not overlooking some of the most important issues already uncovered by the scientific community. We especially examined research in the areas of personality, individual attachment styles, coping approaches individuals employ when confronted with problems, subjective well-being/happiness, life and job satisfaction, and organizational climate.

Upon completion of the theoretical review, we were able to capitalize on our insight, knowledge, and experiences by transforming this into a new battery of questions aimed at capturing the issues that are dealt with in *Why Loyalty Matters*.

It was very important to us to provide a scientifically sound and valid tool. In fact, some of those involved in creating this tool hold doctoral degrees from leading educational institutions and are very familiar with the process of scientific inquiry. We strongly believe our scientific approach to the development of this tool, coupled with practical applications, differentiates our work from others.

Was LoyaltyAdvisor Tested on Other People?

Yes! Absolutely! As with any model, empirical testing is required to prove it works. In fact, we tested our LoyaltyAdvisor model with thousands of people all over the world.

What Approaches Were Used to Design LoyaltyAdvisor?

We started off with a large number of questions about what we were trying to measure. We narrowed our pool of questions to a more manageable number by eliminating irrelevant ones. A statistical approach allowed us to narrow the battery further into overarching dimensions of human behavior.

Based on the questions that described these dimensions, we labeled them accordingly.

Next, the relationships of these dimensions with outcomes such as happiness were explored using statistical techniques. As such, we were able to determine which aspects of our relationship styles and loyalties have the potential to impact satisfaction and happiness.

How Are Scores for LoyaltyAdvisor Calculated?

The scores are calculated on a pre-determined algorithm based on the statistical analyses conducted. These analyses help us construct a score and determine which responses we should use to calculate this score. All these numerical calculations are based on the responses to the LoyaltyAdvisor questions. After you complete your responses, you'll receive a report on the results of these questions.

In the end, there are no value judgments, no saying "you're doing it right here" or "you're doing it wrong there." We simply tell you where your strongest and weakest attributes lie. However, you won't be left without a sense of how urgently you might want to address some of the issues most important for you as highlighted by LoyaltyAdvisor. Therefore, we will benchmark you in relation to people who ranked in the top 15 percent of life satisfaction.

This comparison is not meant to place a judgment that you should or shouldn't do something about a given attribute—you decide what is most important to your life and your self-image. Rather, the benchmark serves to highlight the areas that are more likely to play a role in your happiness.

How Do You Know That LoyaltyAdvisor Is a Reliable Measurement Instrument?

What makes a tool reliable? Well, if it is measuring what it is supposed to measure, then reliability is considered high. It is possible to assess statistically how reliable a survey tool is.

One of the ways to do this is to calculate a statistic that measures internal consistency (called Cronbach's Alpha). This score reflects the degree to which the various questions measure the same factors. If alpha is greater than 0.80, then reliability is high. All the questions we used in this tool have high internal reliability scores!

Can Anyone Use LoyaltyAdvisor?

Anyone with Internet access and the one-time access code located on the reverse side of the dust jacket of this book can complete LoyaltyAdvisor. However, once you've completed the questions, and the report has been generated and emailed to you, your access code will be deactivated.

We hope you have enjoyed *Why Loyalty Matters*. And we hope, too, that you will take a few minutes to try LoyaltyAdvisor. We think you'll find it as powerful as we do.

References

Carver, C. S., Scheier, M. F. and J. K. Weintraub (1989), "Assessing Coping Strategies: A Theoretically Based Approach" *Journal of Personality and Social Psychology*, Vol. 56, No. 2, 267–283.

Diener, E., Suh, E. M., Lucas, R. E. and H. L. Smith (1999), "Subjective Well-Being: Three Decades of Progress" *Psychological Bulletin*, Vol. 125, No. 2, 276–302.

Hazan, C. and P. R. Shaver (1987), "Romantic Love Conceptualized as an Attachment Process" *Journal of Personality and Social Psychology*, Vol. 52, No. 3, 511–524.

McCrae, R. R., and P. T. Costa Jr., (1987), "Validation of the five-factor model of personality across instruments and observers" *Journal of Personality and Social Psychology*, 52, 81–90.

Rusbult, C., Martz, J. M. and C. R. Agnew (1998), "The Investment Model Scale: Measuring commitment level, satisfaction level, quality of alternatives, and investment size" *Personal Relationships*, 357–359.

Acknowledgments

The authors are convinced that the circumstances and events that brought us together to write *Why Loyalty Matters* were a gift from God. So it is only fitting that we begin by giving thanks to God for bringing us together and for the many blessings in our lives.

Tim and Lerzan would like to give a special thanks to Luke Williams, their co-author. Luke's relationship with this book began with his willingness to review very early drafts of chapters we had written. His reviews and suggestions were so extensive and brilliant that we recruited him to be our editor. Within days, however, it became apparent that we had uncovered much more than an editor—we had found a powerful co-author. More important, we had found someone who we are certain is a lifelong friend.

Luke would like to offer special thanks to his lifelong friends, Tim and Lerzan, for their wisdom, guidance, and friendship. This amazing journey would be impossible without you.

We must acknowledge a few legendary thinkers, because this book would not be possible without the pioneering efforts of these brilliant individuals, who recognized and advanced the importance of loyalty. Chief among them are the esteemed American philosopher Josiah Royce, Columbia law professor George Fletcher, and the influential economist Albert Hirschman. Their writings on loyalty serve as the standard by which all other works on loyalty will be measured.

We must also acknowledge some truly wonderful people who have put their own blood, sweat, and tears into making this book a success.

We begin by thanking the best book agents on the planet, Michael Ebeling and Kristina Holmes of the Ebeling Agency, and our one-of-a-kind marvelous publisher, Glenn Yeffeth of BenBella. Working with you has been an exceptional experience. Michael, Kristina, and Glenn, thank you so much for your unwavering faith in us and in this book.

Cathy Lewis of C.S. Lewis & Co. Publicists, Kevin Small and Carolyn Monaco of ResultSource, and Adrienne Lang of BenBella—thank you, thank you, thank you for your vision and expertise in helping us get widespread publicity for *Why Loyalty Matters*. We are also indebted to Joel Roberts of Joel D. Roberts and Associates for his wonderful media training and consulting.

To Catherine Martell, Elen Alexov, Manjiri Patwardhan, Brett Tucker, and Tony Cosentino of Ipsos Loyalty, thank you for your untiring efforts to get this book into the hands of everyone. You are simply fantastic.

It is impossible to thank all of the people who provided support in the writing of this book. However, the contributions of several individuals and companies have been invaluable in completing this book.

We wish to thank all of our colleagues at Ipsos Loyalty, Fordham University, and Koç University, whose talent, imagination, and dedication are a fountain of inspiration. We especially want to thank Anna Koren, Manjiri Patwardhan, Nancy Costopoulos, Rosita Mathew, Marina Gudovich, and Anna Sohail of Ipsos Loyalty for their review and contributions to a series of drafts as this book took shape, which greatly aided in the quality of the final manuscript. Additionally, we would like to thank Eli Finkel and Arya Abedin for their superb guidance and subject matter expertise, acting as unpaid editors for key chapters.

We want to thank Didier Truchot, Jean-Marc Lech, Henri Wallard, Liz Musch, Matt McNerny, Gailynn Nicks, Antoine Moreau, Catherine Martell, Simon Atkinson, Mustapha Tabba, José Roberto Labinas, Steve Levy, Antoine Solom, Pascal Bourgeat, Marco Salamon, Gregoire De Monplanet, Pedro Nevado, Dietmar Puppendahl, Jerome Foltier, Hector Jaso Guerro, Sean Liu, Sidar Gedik, Alexandre de Saint Leon, Marle Manse, Eveline Duquesne, Ken Peterson,

Nancy Costopoulos, Curt Carlson, Jeff Repace, Bob Daly, Kathy Perrier, Alexander Buoye, Julie Berg, Brett Tucker, Sharan Duggal, Pierre Turenne, and Tony Cosentino of Ipsos Loyalty for believing passionately that loyalty is vital to the success of both companies and individuals. We very much appreciate your support and faith in us as we wrote *Why Loyalty Matters*. We would also like to thank Howard Tuckman, Donna Rapaccioli, Victor Borun, Alfred Holden, Sertan Kabadayi, Hooman Estelami, Dawn Lerman, Marcia Flicker, Larry King, Al Greco, Michael Chattalas, Luke Kachersky, and Sarah Maxwell at Fordham University and Attila Askar, Yaman Arkun, Baris Tan, Ebru Tan, Zeynep Gurhan Canli, Esra Gencturk, Aysegul Ozsomer, Serdar Sayman, Skander Esseghaier, Nilufer Aydinoglu, Ayten Kok, Atakan Yalcin, Evrim Gunes, and Deniz Aksen at Koç University for their continued support and for being wonderful colleagues.

Our thanks go to Alex Lutskiy, Bala Subbiah, Saurabh Zadgaonkar, and Alex Buoye for their insights in the development of LoyaltyAdvisor. A special thank you to Miray Kurtay for the long hours he dedicated to the development of our Web site and the deployment of LoyaltyAdvisor.

As this book touches on the role that a single individual can play in shaping the lives of others, we want to thank several people who were instrumental in helping us become who we are today. While the care and concern of innumerable individuals have helped to shape who we are, the friendship and guidance of some in particular holds immeasurable significance. In this regard, Tim would like to thank Roland Rust, Tony Zahorik, Bruce Cooil, Stephen Clemens, Ken Peterson, Ted Chen, Tiffany Perkins-Munn, Demitry Estrin, Jared Shellaway, Bill Heim, Terry Vavra, Doug Pruden, Bill Dunn, Heather Kowalczyk, Susan Boche, Heather Evans, V. Kumar, Vikas Mittal, Tor Wallin Andreassen, Jay Kandampully, A. "Parsu" Parasuraman, Katherine Lemon, Ruth Bolton, Ben Schneider, Chester Elton, Tom Markert, Jose Miguel "Cote" Salinas, Tim Brown, Jim Welch, Tom Kessler, Tom D'Orazio, Peter Jueptner, Keithe Williams, Steve Roberts, Tommy Bell, Barry Edwards, Ed Routon, Jim Alcott, Roger Ferguson, Loftin McCormick, Art Chesler, Thomas Earl Keiningham, and Cebert Carden. Lerzan would like to thank her dearest friends, Sebnem Avsar and Ahu Parlar, for always being there for her! You are amazing. And an extraordinary thanks goes to Billur Sakintuna, Ozlem Tekin, Ozge Koray, Sara Boratav, and Namita Bhatnagar for greatly enriching Lerzan's life. Special thanks also go to Sina Avsar, Ibrahim Ozay, Arzu Wasti, Meric Demirkol, Sedef Celik, Reyhan Kayabas, Esra Edin, Aylin Buyuk, Suhnaz Yilmaz, Demet Yalcin Mousseau, Ulgen Akin, Guliz Elbi, Reside Taskin, Selin Sol, Yaprak and Can Adamoglu, Ebru Engin, Ergem and Ozgur Tohumcu, Bart Lariviere, Isabelle Van Eersel, Filiz Kurtay, Arican Kurtay, Mine Kurtay, and Melisa Kurtay for always providing delight in our lives. A special thank you to our talented photographer and friend Goknur Olguner and Eleven Hearts Photography for the wonderful pictures and Guven Baltaci for making us look beautiful. Luke would like to thank his closest friends (especially for tolerating him during his disappearing act): Alex Anievas, Vincent Randazzo, Andy Weck, Rick Dowling, Jason Millo, Justin Orenstein, Matt Durey, Steve Martin, Stephanie Entis, Michelle Willner, Claire Stretch, Sarah Lawrence, Greg Dixon, and Becky Scherzer. If just one of you had not been a part of our lives, we are certain that our lives would have been much less fruitful, and much less happy.

Luke would also like to add "Rest in Peace" for Matt Gibney. His writing efforts on this book were done with you at heart.

We end by giving the greatest thanks to our families, who have endured the unrewarding task of providing emotional support and encouragement while the authors spent many long nights squirreled away writing and unable to reciprocate. To Hana Keiningham, Sage Keiningham, Lillie Keiningham, Titus Keiningham, Katrin Keiningham, Alexander Keiningham, Christopher Keiningham, Ihsan Aksoy, Levent Aksoy, Pelin Kurtay, Miray Kurtay, Deren Kurtay, George Williams, Katherine Williams, Scott Williams, and Shelley Reiner, thank you for your love, patience, and understanding—and most importantly, for allowing us to follow our calling.

Index

About the Authors

Timothy Keiningham and **Lerzan Aksoy** are two of the world's most highly acclaimed loyalty experts. Tim is global chief strategy officer at Ipsos Loyalty, one of the world's largest market research firms. Lerzan is associate professor at Fordham University in New York City.

Tim was recognized as having contributed one of the top twenty scientific papers in the field of marketing over the past twenty-five years. **Lerzan** was recognized as the top young scientist of 2007 in Turkey by the Junior Chamber International (TOYP Award for Scientific Leadership).

Tim and **Lerzan**'s prior book, *Loyalty Myths*, was ranked as the number four best business book of 2006 by *The Globe and Mail* newspaper (Toronto, Canada), one of the thirty best business books of 2006 by Soundview Executive Book Summaries, and a 2007 finalist for the Berry-AMA Book Prize for Best Book in Marketing.

Their groundbreaking research on the importance of loyalty has received over a dozen prestigious scientific awards. For their research together, they have been awarded:

Marketing Science Institute/H. Paul Root Award from the *Journal of Marketing* for the article judged to represent the most significant contribution to the advancement of the practice of marketing,

Citations of Excellence "Top 50" Award (top 50 management papers of approximately 20,000 papers reviewed that year) from Emerald Management Reviews,

Outstanding Paper Award (best paper) from the journal *Managing Service Quality* two years in a row (2007 and 2008).

Internationally renowned speakers, consultants, and authors, **Tim** and **Lerzan** live in the New York metropolitan area.

Luke Williams is senior project manager at Ipsos Loyalty, where he leads the day-to-day activity of large-scale, international loyalty engagements for the firm. A prolific writer, **Luke** has published articles in journals such as *Quirks Marketing Research Review, Journal of Database Marketing & Customer Strategy Management,* and *School of Government and International Affairs Review.* **Luke** received a master's degree in Social Research Methods from the University of Durham (U.K.) and a bachelor's degree in Sociology from Rutgers University (U.S.).